Metaphor, Ritual, and Order in John 12–13

This book offers new interpretative insight into the Gospel of John, applying a combination of critical discourse analysis, conceptual metaphor theory, and anthropological theories of ritual.

Specifically it explores the meaning of the statement "Now the ruler of this world will be driven out" in John 12:31 and defends a widely overlooked alternative reading. The author proposes a prophecy-fulfilment scheme whereby this predictive utterance by Jesus is subsequently implied as fulfilled in the departure of the satanically-possessed Judas from the circle of Jesus' disciples at the Last Supper in John 13:30. Addressing several major strands relating to purity, exorcism, and group identity, the analysis provides an important entry-point for a fresh examination of the Fourth Gospel as a whole. The book represents a significant contribution to Johannine scholarship and to New Testament studies and will be of interest to scholars of religion, theology and biblical studies.

Todd E. Klutz is Senior Lecturer in Biblical Studies at the University of Manchester, UK.

Routledge Interdisciplinary Perspectives on Biblical Criticism

Epistemology and Biblical Theology
From the Pentateuch to Mark's Gospel
Dru Johnson

Thinking Sex with the Great Whore
Deviant Sexualities and Empire in the Book of Revelation
Luis Menéndez-Antuña

A Philosophical Theology of the Old Testament
A historical, experimental, comparative and analytic perspective
Jaco Gericke

Human Agency and Divine Will
The Book of Genesis
Charlotte Katzoff

Paul and Diversity
A New Perspective on Σάρξ and Resilience in Galatians
Linda Joelsson

A Prototype Approach to Hate and Anger in the Hebrew Bible
Conceiving Emotions
Deena Grant

Metaphor, Ritual, and Order in John 12–13
Judas and the Prince
Todd E. Klutz

For more information about this series, please visit: https://www.routledge.com/Routledge-Interdisciplinary-Perspectives-on-Biblical-Criticism/book-series/RIPBC

Metaphor, Ritual, and Order in John 12–13
Judas and the Prince

Todd E. Klutz

LONDON AND NEW YORK

First published 2024
by Routledge
4 Park Square, Milton Park, Abingdon, Oxon OX14 4RN

and by Routledge
605 Third Avenue, New York, NY 10158

Routledge is an imprint of the Taylor & Francis Group, an informa business

© 2024 Todd E. Klutz

The right of Todd E. Klutz to be identified as authors of this work has been asserted in accordance with sections 77 and 78 of the Copyright, Designs and Patents Act 1988.

All rights reserved. No part of this book may be reprinted or reproduced or utilised in any form or by any electronic, mechanical, or other means, now known or hereafter invented, including photocopying and recording, or in any information storage or retrieval system, without permission in writing from the publishers.

Trademark notice: Product or corporate names may be trademarks or registered trademarks, and are used only for identification and explanation without intent to infringe.

British Library Cataloguing-in-Publication Data
A catalogue record for this book is available from the British Library

ISBN: 978-1-032-39451-0 (hbk)
ISBN: 978-1-032-41699-1 (pbk)
ISBN: 978-1-003-35931-9 (ebk)

DOI: 10.4324/9781003359319

Typeset in Times New Roman
by MPS Limited, Dehradun

Contents

	Preface	*vi*
	List of Acronyms and Abbreviations	*vii*
1	'Down' and 'Out' in Scholarly Readings of John 12:31	1
2	Metaphor and Exorcism in John 12–13	10
3	Exorcism, Meal, and Morsel in John 12–13	34
4	Disorder, Discipline, and Eucharist in John 6–13	60
5	Conclusion	84
	Bibliography	*95*
	Index	*101*

Preface

The writing of the present book began with a short academic paper entitled 'The Story of Judas in the Gospel of John', presented at the 'Love, Boundaries and Sacred Texts: Methods and Case Studies' colloquium organised by the Centre of Biblical Studies at the University of Manchester, and convened at the Universities of Manchester and Chester, 2–3 May 2019. Feedback from other participants at the colloquium and a semester of research leave in 2021 helped me to develop the paper into the present study. More recently, postgraduate seminar groups at the Universities of Manchester and Gloucestershire have responded to presentations of the same research and enabled me to improve its argument. For helpful conversation at various stages in the writing process, special gratitude is owed to Catrin Williams, Christos Papageorgiou, George Brooke, Peter Oakes, Andy Boakye, David Lamb, Stephen Barton, Elizabeth Shively, Philip Esler, Andrew Lincoln, Francis Watson, Sarah Parkhouse, Michael Hoelzl, and Graham Twelftree. If the book facilitates further conversation with each of them in the days ahead, it will have achieved one of its highest purposes.

Acronyms and Abbreviations

G. Phil	*Gospel of Philip*
IG II	*Inscriptiones Atticae Euclidis anno posteriors*, vol. 2, edited by J. Kirchener *et al.*
NHC	Nag Hammadi Codex
PApoll	*Papyrus grecs d'Apollônos Anô*, edited by R. Rémondon.
3PLond	*Greek Papyri in the British Museum*, vol. 3, edited by F. G. Kenyon and H. I. Bell.
1PTebt 33	Tebtunis papyrus 33, 'Preparations for a Roman Visitor', in *The Tebtunis Papyri*, vol. 1 part 1, edited by B. P. Grenfell, A. S. Hunt, and J. G. Smylie.
P. Ryl. Greek Add	*John Rylands Additional (i.e., Unpublished) Greek Papyri*
RW	The Johannine 'ruler of this world' (i.e., Satan)
VA	Flavius Philostratus, *Vita Apollonii* = *The Life of Apollonius of Tyana*

1 'Down' and 'Out' in Scholarly Readings of John 12:31

Critical Reflections on a Couple of Normal Interpretations

In scholarly commentary on the Gospel of John, the utterance attributed to Jesus in verse 31 of the Gospel's twelfth chapter – 'Now the ruler of this world will be driven out' (νῦν ὁ ἄρχων τοῦ κόσμου τούτου ἐκβληθήσεται ἔξω) – is normally interpreted as referring to either one or the other of the following postulated results of Jesus' approaching crucifixion: either the ruler is to be cast down from heaven and thus also, presumably, away from the divine presence;[1] or he is to be driven out of the 'world' in the sense that the divine judgement about to take place in the cross will increasingly limit the power of Satan to influence believers.[2] Other interpretative issues have been raised in connection with the same clause – who or what, for instance, should be identified as the 'ruler of this world'?[3] – and are given due attention in careful readings of the text; but central to the interests of the present study are, first, the question implicit in the two interpretations just summarised – out of what, exactly, is the ruler of this world to be expelled? – but also whether a widely overlooked third reading may possess greater merit than has been recognised since it was first proposed several decades ago.

At least one source of motivation for this sort of inquiry is worth mentioning before proceeding further. In brief, both of the familiar scholarly readings just noted are burdened with heavy liabilities many of which have been recognised in published exegesis.[4] As noted, for instance, by Wilhelm Thüsing over fifty years ago, if Jesus' utterance in John 12:31 should be taken as referring to a vertical relocation of Satan downward, it would be the only instance in the Fourth Gospel where either the devil or any other evil spirit is conceptualised as experiencing movement downward in space from some assumed position above, either from heaven or from some unspecified location.[5] Instead of moving up or down, along an assumed vertical axis, the various evil powers depicted in the Fourth Gospel are closely tied to human characters and events on a horizontal plane;[6] any processes of relocation they experience are implied to involve movement either into or out of one metaphorical container or another (e.g., a group of people or an individual character in the story).[7]

Nonetheless, the Lukan account of Jesus' vision of Satan falling like lightning from heaven (Lk. 10:18) is often cited as comparative evidence for inferring downward movement in John 12:31. Against that argument, the same account derives much of its force as a reflection on exorcistic victories summarised directly beforehand in Luke (10:1, 9, 17), and thus on a type of activity normally assumed to be missing from the Fourth Gospel.[8] Judged as comparative evidence for clarifying the meaning of John 12:31, therefore, the Lukan Jesus' reference to the fall of Satan is severely limited in value by the absence of Synoptic-style exorcisms in the Fourth Gospel;[9] and similar appeals either to the descent of the vanquished dragon to land and sea in Rev. 12:12, or to the poorly attested variant reading βληθήσεται κάτω ('he will be thrown down') in John 12:31b, are plagued by equally serious shortcomings.[10] Being thrown out and being thrown down, to be sure, are not completely different ideas; but they are significantly different, and the significance of 'the ruler of this world' being thrown out in the Fourth Gospel is very weighty for that writing's portrayal of Jesus, Judas, the other disciples, and the satanic ruler, as the analysis below will show.

The most commonly suggested alternative – that the location from which the ruler will be removed is the κόσμος (the 'world'),[11] understood in the same negative sense with which the term is used in the first clause of John 12:31 – is burdened by a largely different set of problems whose cumulative force is at least as great as those affecting the position just summarised. For instance, since the narrator of the Gospel has already portrayed Jesus several times as a legitimate prophet whose predictions prove in every case to be reliable,[12] the Gospel's audience would have reason to expect that at some point after John 12:31b 'the ruler of this world' will be described as withdrawing from the world if indeed that is how Jesus' prediction is best understood. Yet in every subsequent passage where the ruler (understood as the devil or Satan) is mentioned, he is portrayed either explicitly or implicitly as still active in 'this world', the world 'below';[13] and although he can be understood as present in the satanically possessed Judas when the latter is portrayed in John 13:30 as withdrawing from the Jesus circle, the place that Judas vacates in that context is scarcely to be understood as 'the world', as the analysis below demonstrates. As a result, the idea that the Gospel's audience is being prompted by the text to expect the place vacated by the ruler to be 'the world' does not cohere with the relatively clear and direct style of the Gospel's efforts elsewhere to portray Jesus as a prophet whose predictions always turn out to come demonstrably true; and farther along in the analysis below, other considerations will emerge that only strengthen the case against the 'world' interpretation.

A Neglected Alternative: Wilhelm Thüsing on John 12:31

As already hinted, there is an interesting and potentially very attractive alternative to the two troubled readings just described. After confronting head-on some of the difficulties just summarised, the aforementioned Wilhelm Thüsing proposed that the location from which the ruler in John 12:31 would be expunged should be identified as the circle of Jesus' disciples understood as a community, with the nocturnal departure of Judas from the subsequent meal in John 13:30 corresponding to the eviction projected by Jesus in 12:31.[14] A substantial part of the communicative effect of such a reading is encapsulated nicely in Thüsing's words:

> There is now a community of people in which Satan no longer has a place, from which he can be expelled; and indeed, it exists through the exaltation [i.e., of Jesus]. The elimination of the betrayer is a real picture of this matter.[15]

Thüsing's understanding of the expulsion anticipated in 12:31 as realised in the departure of the satanically possessed Judas from the Jesus circle in 13:30 has potential for development into an interpretative synthesis superior to the more familiar alternatives; and much of what follows in the present study is devoted precisely to giving Thüsing's idea the fuller articulation I think it deserves.

The need for a more comprehensive statement of Thüsing's position arises partly from the brevity of his own presentation of it. His comments on the matter are limited to part of a single footnote in his monograph and thus afford neither a full elaboration of his proposal nor even a brief defence of it.[16] This backgrounding of his own view of the matter may help explain why Thüsing's position is dismissed so casually in the late Rudolf Schnackenburg's commentary on John's Gospel, in which Thüsing is singled out as the lone target of Schnackenburg's comment that a 'reference to Judas' departure from the group of the Twelve', in John 12:31b, 'is hardly likely'.[17] In support of that judgement, Schnackenburg asserts that Thüsing's proposal is inconsistent with John's strong 'interest in the salvation of men',[18] not merely as individuals but as a group. But Schnackenburg never specifies precisely what it is about Thüsing's reading that results in an underestimation of the Fourth Gospel's collectivism; and as indicated in the analysis below, since Thüsing's interpretation entails that Judas has become a dangerous threat to the purity and safety of the Jesus circle as a whole by the time he withdraws from the group in 13:30, it implicitly conceptualises the relocation of Judas in the latter reference as a purification event that saves Jesus' followers as a group from a diabolical agent of unbelief, discord, and pollution – an event which therefore scarcely conflicts with the soteriological collectivism inferred by Schnackenburg from the Fourth Gospel more generally.

Although Schnackenburg's comments on John 12:31 overlook the potential of Thüsing's suggestion to reinforce some of Schnackenburg's own interpretative judgements, he at least shows awareness that Thüsing's proposal constitutes a distinct alternative worthy of scholarly consideration, however brief. The same compliment, however, cannot be properly extended to many other scholarly works published in Johannine studies since the appearing of the second edition of Thüsing's monograph (1970); indeed, none of the many relevant publications consulted by the present writer goes as far as Schnackenburg does towards an adequate appreciation of Thüsing's contribution. Insofar as critical commentaries are expected to engage both with a range of exegetical options and with a generous selection of relevant scholarly studies on the portions of biblical text they treat, students of the Fourth Gospel might expect esteemed commentaries such as those by K. Wengst, H. Thyen, A. T. Lincoln, D. A. Carson, U. Schnelle, F. Moloney, M. Edwards, G. Beasley-Murray, C. K. Barrett, R. Brown, and R. Bultmann either to engage at least briefly with Thüsing in particular (wherever his work antedates theirs by more than a year or two) on John 12:31 or perhaps even to entertain a similar interpretation they may have conjectured on their own. As it happens, that is not the case;[19] and various other, non-commentary, types of scholarship whose particular statements of focus would justify at least brief comment on Thüsing's perspective or related possibilities prove to be comparably lacking in that particular respect,[20] whatever value they afford in other ways.

The Promise of a New Approach

The aforementioned dearth of scholarly engagement with Wilhelm Thüsing's alternative exegesis of John 12:31 represents a more far-reaching misjudgement than it might seem; for, as argued below, interpreting Jesus' utterance in John 12:31b as a prediction whose realisation is implicitly identified in John 13:30 as the withdrawal of Judas from the Christ group has implications that extend beyond the limits of a few clauses of Greek text. Indeed, the prophecy-fulfilment scheme elaborated in the pages below has potential to impact everything from our understanding of the Fourth Gospel's portrayal of Jesus, Judas, Peter, and other characters in the narrative, to the cohesion, coherence, theology, rhetorical force, ritual assumptions, and sociopolitical context of the Fourth Gospel as a whole. More specifically, by highlighting reference chains and lexical strings that tie nearly all of John 13 to various parts of its antecedent co-text (especially 12:28–31 but also 6:60–71 and 12:1–8), where either anticipated exorcistic actions or group meals are salient in the text, the proposed schematic structure has the effect of raising the prominence of ritual and symbolic action – not only exorcistic activity but also rules of behaviour for participants at association banquets, and appropriate penalties for unruly conduct in those settings – narrated in the key passages.

A noteworthy consequence of giving due attention to ritual-like activities in the given context is that it enables many of the utterances and actions of Jesus in John 12:31 and 13:1–30 to be interpreted not merely as broadly exorcistic but also as goal-oriented behaviour designed to remove Judas, as an uncooperative presence inimical to the survival of the group, from the Jesus circle. A second and closely related result is that, since the little morsel of food introduced by Jesus and given to Judas in John 13:26–30 plays an instrumental role in both the exorcistic rite and the banquet drama, with its disciplinary climax, it is given much richer significance in the analysis below than in the standard treatments; more particularly, both the size of the morsel and the timing of its provision, relative to other happenings in the meal-symposium sequence of John 13–17, are singled out below as indicators of the Johannine Jesus appraisal of Judas status in the Christ association.

The analysis below does not rely exclusively on any single method or approach familiar in the field of biblical studies. More specifically, although the present study has its origins partly in a separate inquiry making heavy use of redaction-critical and related methods for purposes of understanding the absence of Synoptic-style exorcisms in the Gospel of John,[21] those methods have only proved to be of modest value for illuminating certain features of John 12–13, and most especially the relationship between the satanological material in the meal-footwashing narrative (John 13:1–30) and the Gospel's clearest reference to an exorcistic event, namely, Jesus' antecedent reference to an imminent expulsion of 'the ruler of this world' (John 12:31b). For purposes of dealing with that question, the methodology known as 'Critical Discourse Analysis' (CDA) has demonstrated far greater power for describing, interpreting, and explaining the ways in which the key passages just mentioned are interrelated and combined to form larger structures of discourse in their various levels of context. Owing much to the published research of British linguist Norman Fairclough, and influenced by the systemic-functional linguistics of M. A. K. Halliday and several of his students,[22] CDA emphasises the prominent role played in multi-clausal units of discourse by linguistic phenomena such as 'lexical strings' and 'reference chains', which not only contribute much to the sense of cohesion in a text but also prompt interpreters to infer meaning from the constitutive links. In the ensuing chapters of analysis, for example, a highly meaningful reference chain is inferred which identifies the departure of Judas as narrated in John 13:30 as the event predicted by Jesus back in John 12:31. Of course, like many other reference chains and nearly everything else in textual analysis, that particular chain will require explanation, defence, and interpretation; but one of the numerous merits of CDA, like the systemic approach which informs it, is that it provides students of language and discourse with a linguistically informed toolkit, a powerful set of heuristic concepts, which enable the critic to see various kinds of potentially meaningful phenomena that without the toolkit could easily be overlooked.

A few other features of CDA help to explain its appeal for use in the present study. As a work of inquiry within the field of New Testament studies, the present investigation is produced with a desire that it be intelligible and useful to other scholars and students whose interest in the same field is likely to be stronger than their interest in linguistics or method and theory in the study of religion. In that connection, the hospitality of CDA to insights from a wide range of other approaches to textual interpretation, including those with a longer history of use in biblical scholarship (e.g., socio-rhetorical criticism), is an important virtue;[23] but almost as vital for purposes of the present study, CDA includes ample space for engagement with recent cognitive-linguistic theorising in regard to 'conceptual metaphor'.[24] In the chapters that follow, George Lakoff and Mark Johnson's influential thinking about the conceptual differences between 'container metaphors' and 'orientational metaphors' helps not only to identify why the driving 'out' of the satanic ruler in John 12:31 is significantly different from the casting 'down' of Satan in Rev. 12:7–12 but also to highlight a noteworthy instance of metaphorical coherence in reading the container metaphor in John 12:31 as anticipating the outgoing of the satanically possessed Judas later in the Gospel narrative (13:30). Wherever critical concepts adapted from these theorists and others significantly impact the present inquiry, they will be discussed with a view to clarifying their relevance to that particular stage in the analysis.

Notes

1 See, e.g., K. Wengst, *Das Johannes-evangelium, 2. Teilband: Kapitel 11–21*, 2nd edn, TKNT (Stuttgart: Verlag W. Kohlhammer, 2001), 75–76; J. Kovacs, '"Now Shall the Ruler of This World Be Driven Out": Jesus Death as Cosmic Battle in John 12:20–36', *JBL* 114 (2, 1995): 238; and D. A. Carson, *The Gospel According to John* (Leicester: Inter-Varsity Press; Grand Rapids: William B. Eerdmans, 1991), 443.

2 See, e.g., A. Reinhartz, *The Word in the World: The Cosmological Tale in the Fourth Gospel*, SBLMS 42 (Atlanta: Scholars Press, 1992), 111; R. Schnackenburg, *The Gospel according to John*, vol. 2, trans. Cecily Hastings et al., HTKNT (Tunbridge Wells, Kent: Burns & Oates, 1971), 392; R. E. Brown, *The Gospel According to John I-XII*, AB 29 (Garden City: Doubleday, 1966), 477; and R. Bultmann, *The Gospel of John: A Commentary*, trans. G. R. Beasley-Murray (Oxford: Basil Blackwell, 1971), 431.

3 Understood in the present study, as by most commentators, to be identical to 'the devil'/'Satan'/'the evil one' (8:44; 13:2, 27; 17:15); see, e.g., A. T. Lincoln, *The Gospel According to Saint John* (Peabody: Hendrickson; London: Continuum, 2005), 352; and H. Thyen, *Das Johannes-evangelium*, HzNT 6 (Tübingen: Mohr-Siebeck, 2005), pp. 636–37; but taken by M. B. Ali, '"The Ruler" in the Fourth Gospel', *Biblica et Patristica Thoruniensia* 12 (2019): 16–22, as referring to Jesus; and by T. Thatcher, *Greater Than Caesar: Christology and Empire in the Fourth Gospel* (Minneapolis: Fortress, 2008), 116–17, as denoting Caesar.
4 Particularly helpful discussion of the scholarly positions is given by R. A. Piper, 'Satan, Demons, and the Absence of Exorcism in the Fourth Gospel', in *Christology, Controversy, and Community: New Testament Essays in Honour of David R. Catchpole*, ed. D. G. Horrell and C. M. Tuckett (Leiden: Brill, 2000), 271–76.
5 W. Thüsing, *Die Erhöhung und Verherrlichung Jesu im Johannesevangelium*, 2nd edn, NTAbh 21.1 (Münster: Aschendorff, 1970), 22 n. 43, who judges the 'parallel' in Lk. 10:18 as inadequate for inferring a fall of the ruler from heaven in John 12:31.
6 As highlighted, e.g., by E. Pagels, *The Origin of Satan* (London: Penguin, 1995), 100–102, 105–106, 111; and defended below.
7 On the function of container metaphors in language and thought generally, see G. Lakoff and M. Johnson, *Metaphors We Live By* (Chicago: University of Chicago Press, 1980), 3–6, 29–32. For purposes of the present study, the basic insight is that our everyday experience of embodiment gives us an 'in-out' orientation exemplified by our habit of imposing conceptual boundaries where no natural boundary exists. The bushes 'into' which my neighbour's children threw the bottle is not a clearly bounded container; nor is the college 'out of' which several students were expelled last year for antisocial behaviour. As Lakoff and Johnson explain, the phenomenon is not merely a matter of linguistic expression but of cognition itself.
8 Piper, 'The Absence of Exorcism', 253–63; and G. H. Twelftree, *In the Name of Jesus: Exorcism among Early Christians* (Grand Rapids: Baker, 2007), 183–205, are useful surveys of scholarship up to around 2000 and 2007 respectively. More recent developments on related matters, especially the political overtones of demonological motifs in the Fourth Gospel, are explored by N. T. Wright with J. P. Davies, 'John, Jesus, and "The Ruler of This World": Demonic Politics in the Fourth Gospel', *Conception, Reception, and the Spirit: Essays in Honour of Andrew T. Lincoln*, ed. J. G. McConville and L. K. Pietersen (Eugene: Cascade, 2015), 71–89.
9 In the analysis below, I suggest that previous treatments of the problem have tended to weaken their own analytical power by assuming that the best definition of 'exorcism' is a narrow and tightly bounded one; but that same critique leaves fully intact the verticality/container distinction discussed above in connection with John 12:31 and Lk. 10:17. My critique here of stressing similarities between John 12:31 and Lk. 10:17 does not entail a low estimation of redaction-critical and related approaches to studying the Fourth Gospel's appropriation of earlier gospel-traditions involving exorcism, a matter about which more is said above under the heading 'The Promise of an Alternative Approach'.
10 E.g., alongside the similarities noted by Kovacs, 'Jesus' Death as Cosmic Battle', 238, between John 12:31 and the apocalyptic scene of combat in Rev. 12:7–9, there is also the contrast between the defeated dragon in Rev. 12:12 coming down (κατέβη) and the ruler in John 12:31 being driven out

(ἐκβληθήσεται ἔξω). As for the variants attested for the final two words of John 12:31, βλήθησεται ἔξω has the support of p[66] and D while preserving the force of the container metaphor; whereas βληθήσεται κάτω invites comparison to Lk. 10:18 and Rev. 12:7–12 but is best explained as assimilation to those texts and has only weak external evidence (q, the Sinaitic Syriac, the Sahidic tradition, and Epiphanius) in its favour; cf. C. K. Barrett, *The Gospel According to John: An Introduction with Commentary and Notes on the Greek Text*, 2nd edn (London: SPCK, 1978), 427.
11 For a few exemplary proponents, see n. 2 above.
12 See, e.g., John 2:18–22; 4:16–19; 6:5–14, 64; 11:23–45; 18:32; and the correspondences between 13:21–26 and 18:2–14; and between the prophecy in 13:38 and the events narrated in 18:15–27.
13 See John 14:30; 16:11; 17:12, 15; and 18:2–5.
14 Thüsing, *Die Erhöhung und Verherrlichung Jesu*, 22 n. 43.
15 Ibid., my translation of Thüsing's 'Es gibt jetzt eine Gemeinschaft von Menschen, in der der Satan keinen Platz mehr hat, aus der er verwiesen werden kann; und zwar gibt es sie durch die Erhöhung; die Ausscheidung des Verräters ist ein reales 'Bild' für diesen Sachverhalt' (Thüsing, p. 22 n. 43).
16 Ibid.
17 Schnackenburg, *The Gospel according to John*, vol. 2, 392. Readers unfamiliar with Thüsing's monograph but tempted to extend Schnackenburg's judgement to Thüsing's book as a whole would do well to consider first a review published by the late J. F. McHugh, former Dean of the Theology Faculty at the University of Durham, who praised the first edition of Thüsing's work (1960) as 'the best study of St. John's Gospel I have ever read: one can only urge others to buy and to read it – several times'; McHugh, review of W. Thüsing, *Die Erhöhung und Verherrlichung Jesu im Johannesevangelium*, NTAbh 21 (Münster: Aschendorffsche, 1960) in *CBQ* 22.4 (1960): 461.
18 Ibid.
19 See Wengst, *Das Johannes-evangelium*, 75–76; Thyen, *Das Johannes-evangelium*, 565–66; Lincoln, *The Gospel According to Saint John*, 352–53; Carson, *The Gospel According to John*, 442–43; U. Schnelle, *Das Evangelium nach Johannes*, 4th edn, THzNT 4 (Leipzig: Evangelische Verlagsanstalt, 2009), 228; F. Moloney, *Signs and Shadows: Reading John 5–12* (Minneapolis: Fortress, 1996), 191–92; M. Edwards, *John*, Blackwell Bible Commentaries (Oxford: Blackwell Publishing, 2004), 127–28; G. Beasley-Murray, *John*, WBC 36 (Waco: Word, 1987), 213–14; Barrett, *The Gospel According to St John*, 426–27; Brown, *The Gospel According to John*, 468, 477; and Bultmann, *The Gospel of John*, 431.
20 See, e.g., M. W. Martin, *Judas and the Rhetoric of Comparison in the Fourth Gospel*, New Testament Monographs 25 (Sheffield: Sheffield Phoenix Press, 2010); W. Pratscher, 'Judas Iskariot im Neuen Testament und im Judas evangelium', *NovT* 52 (2010): 1–23; A.-B. Renger, 'The Ambiguity of Jesus: On the Mythicity of a New Testament Figure', *Literature and Theology* 27.1 (2013), 1–17; C. Bennema, 'Judas the Betrayer: The Black Sheep of the Family', in *Character Studies in the Fourth Gospel: Narrative Approaches to Seventy Figures in John*, ed. S. A. Hunt, D. F. Tolmie, and R. Zimmermann, (WUNT 314; Tübingen: Mohr-Siebeck, 2013), 360–72; G. W. Most, 'The Judas of the Gospels and the *Gospel of Judas*', in *The Gospel of Judas in Context: Proceedings of the First International Congress on the Gospel of Judas, Paris, Sorbonne, October 27th–28th 2006*, ed. M. Scopello (Leiden: E. J. Brill, 2008), 69–80; W. Klassen, *Judas: Betrayer or Friend of Jesus* (Minneapolis: Fortress, 1996); J. M. Robinson, *The Secrets of Judas* (New York:

HarperCollins, 2006); T. Thatcher, 'Jesus, Judas, and Peter: Character by Contrast in the Fourth Gospel', *BSac* 153 (1996): 435–48; and I. de la Potterie, 'L'exaltation du Fils de l'homme', *Gregorianum* 49.3 (1968): 460–78.

21 An inquiry still in progress, clearly related in theme to the present study but kept in the background here, primarily because its conclusions have not yet been reached. However, because source-critical assumptions are unavoidable at a few points in the present work, I would be remiss not to acknowledge my own assumption that, in varying degrees, all three Synoptic Gospels (especially Mark and Luke) are among the sources adapted in the composition of the Fourth Gospel.

22 See especially N. Fairclough, *Language and Power*, 3rd edn (London and New York: Routledge, 2015); Fairclough, *Critical Discourse Analysis*, 2nd edn (London and New York: Routledge, 2013); and Fairclough, *Discourse and Social Change* (Cambridge: Polity, 1992); M. A. K. Halliday and C. Matthiessen, *Halliday's Introduction to Functional Grammar*, 4th edn (London: Routledge, 2014); and S. Eggins, *An Introduction to Systemic Functional Linguistics*, 2nd edn (London: Bloomsbury Academic, 2004). The present study is therefore interested primarily in what light the chosen methods can shed on the meaning of John 12:31b in its literary co-text, not in the historical figure of Judas or recent efforts to reimagine him.

23 Examples of CDA and systemic-functional approaches in New Testament scholarship include T. E. Klutz, *The Exorcism Stories in Luke-Acts: A Sociostylistic Reading*, SNTSMS 129 (Cambridge: Cambridge University Press, 2004); and D. A. Lamb, *Text, Context, and the Johannine Community: A Sociolinguistic Analysis of the Johannine Writings*, LNTS 477 (London: Bloomsbury T & T Clark, 2014), esp. 115–20. For a critique of Fairclough's adaptation of Halliday, see S. E. Porter, 'Is Critical Discourse Analysis Critical', in *Discourse Analysis and the New Testament: Approaches and Results*, ed. S. E. Porter and J. T. Reed (LNTS 170; Sheffield: Sheffield Academic Press, 1999), 47–70.

24 The most influential statement of the theory is Lakoff and Johnson's 1980 work *Metaphors We Live By*; but the theory has been developed further in the same authors' *Philosophy in the Flesh: The Embodied Mind and Its Challenge to Modern Thought* (New York: Basic Books, 1999); G. Fauconnier and M. Turner, *The Way We Think: Conceptual Blending and the Mind's Hidden Complexities* (New York: Basic Books, 2002); M. Johnson, *The Meaning of the Body: Aesthetics of Human Understanding* (Cambridge: Cambridge University Press, 2007); and B. Dancygier and E. Sweetser, *Figurative Language* (Cambridge Textbooks in Linguistics; Cambridge: Cambridge University Press, 2014). Some of the key theoretical insights are explicitly incorporated into a CDA framework by S. Statham, *Critical Discourse Analysis: A Practical Introduction to Power in Language* (London: Routledge, 2022), 139–42.

2 Metaphor and Exorcism in John 12–13

Judas: Unbeliever, Devil, and Container Metaphor

The prominence assigned to Judas in the preceding chapter might seem to demand that the present analysis begin where Judas first appears on the stage of the Fourth Gospel: namely, in John 6:60–71, where Judas is identified as the son of Simon Iscariot (v. 71), as the disciple who would eventually 'betray' Jesus, as an embodiment of diabolical vice (v. 70), and as a figure whose implied association with certain unbelieving disciples (v. 64) suggests that he too, from the perspective of the narrator of the FG, had never truly participated in the trust placed in Jesus by his authentic followers. To be sure, any satisfying interpretation of the portrayal of Judas in the Fourth Gospel would require a fuller analysis of John 6:60–71 and its immediate co-text than is provided here; but because the problem introduced above in connection with John 12:31 has potential to be handled in a way that powerfully affects nearly every aspect of the Johannine characterisation of Judas, the analysis below steps into the flow of John's narrative not at the point of Judas' introduction, in John 6, but instead farther downstream, where the structure and plot of the Gospel begin to make their widely recognised turn from the ending of the 'book of signs' (1:19–12:50) to the beginning of the 'book of glory' (13:1–20:31),[1] at a point where, perhaps because Judas is not explicitly mentioned, his implicit but dangerously impure presence escapes the notice of most commentators,[2] with adverse consequences for understanding John 12–13 and its contribution to the force of the Gospel as a whole.

The 'ruler of this world' (ὁ ἄρχων τοῦ κόσμου τούτου) who, according to Jesus in John 12:31, is to be cast out is understood by most scholarly authorities as a reference to the cosmic power designated later in the Fourth Gospel by nearly the same terminology in John 14:30 and 16:11,[3] by ὁ διάβολος ('the devil') in 13:2,[4] by ὁ σατανᾶς ('Satan') in 13:27, and by ὁ πονηρός ('the evil one') in 17:15.[5] Beyond that understanding, most commentators have little to say. There are, however, other interpreters

DOI: 10.4324/9781003359319-2

who see the referent of ὁ ἄρχων τοῦ κόσμου τούτου as rather less straightforward; and in a recent essay by N. T. Wright and J. P. Davies, the key phrase is taken as signifying not only Satan but also the Roman emperor and the political values of imperial rule.[6] Both of those readings have certain merits, albeit partially different ones, but both are also enfeebled by a certain oversight implied above and detailed in the analysis below: namely, like every modern scholarly construal I am aware of except that proposed by Thüsing, both the satanological reading and the implicitly political one neglect strong linguistic and related evidence for the presence of a schematic structure in John 12–13 whereby the prediction of the ruler's expulsion in 12:31 finds dramatic fulfilment shortly afterwards in the Satan-possessed 's withdrawal from the Jesus circle in 13:30. If, as recommended below, the proposed scheme is furthermore taken as a prompt to infer 'extra meaning' from the 'extra structure' identified at the macrodiscursive level of the Gospel narrative,[7] the reference to the ruler in John 12:31 will cry out to be read as involving not only Satan (as 'the ruler of this world') but also his eventual container, Judas;[8] but almost as importantly, by highlighting the role of Judas in the Fourth Gospel as a metaphorical container for the satanic-ruler figure, the same schematic reading has potential to redeem certain elements of the political interpretation and heighten its plausibility, a point to which I will return below.

But first a case must be made for inferring the proposed scheme. Once that has been done, the implications of the scheme for understanding a range of other issues posed by the Fourth Gospel – the relationship between 'the ruler of this world' and Roman power, the respective roles of the eucharist and Jesus' word in cleansing the community of faith from the impurity of in-group unbelief, the duties of maintaining association norms and good order at festive meals – each of these will be considered at least briefly in turn.

The second clause of John 12:31 – 'now the ruler of this world will be driven out' (νῦν ὁ ἄρχων τοῦ κόσμου τούτου ἐκβληθήσεται ἔξω) – is implicitly understood in scholarly exegesis, regardless of the interpreter's chosen position, as conceptualising the movement of an object through space. Where scholarly disagreement takes place regarding that same clause, it normally involves either the identity and scope of the object to be moved – as noted above, is 'the ruler of this world' identical to Satan? Caesar? Both? Someone/something else? – or the boundaries and identity of the implied area, the metaphorical container, from which the object is to be expelled. Regarding the area to be vacated, at least some readers/hearers will respond: Driven out, yes; but from where, exactly?[9] By contrast, there is near unanimity among exegetes in regard to a conceptually related question, to which the present study will return in due course: namely, when 'the ruler of this world' is eventually expelled, where are readers to imagine him being relocated to? The assumption widely shared in scholarly exegesis, apparently, is that this latter question does not warrant careful analysis of the spatial concepts instantiated in the text,[10] an assumption resulting in missed interpretative opportunities that are approached differently below.

A more illuminating approach to this and related questions can, however, be initiated here by offering a single reflection on all the published scholarly opinion the present writer has read concerning the meaning of John 12:31 in its literary context. In brief, none of the relevant exegesis demonstrates either an interest in the possible presence of metaphor(s) in the key line or, more specifically, an awareness of the interpretative tools that Lakoff and Johnson's theory of conceptual metaphor offers the exegete confronted by utterances such as that in John 12:31b. The analytical value of one of those tools – namely, what Lakoff and Johnson call 'orientational metaphor'[11] – can be seen in its capacity for helping us to identify at least one misstep commonly taken in scholarship on John 12:31b, and to understand why it is ill-advised.

The misstep in question has been mentioned briefly above, in connection with Thüsing's interpretation, but was not assessed in that context from the perspective of conceptual metaphor theory, which is used here to identify the difficulty more clearly. The difficulty is to be seen in the widely repeated suggestion that the reference in John 12:31b to the expulsion of the ruler is best understood as a parallel not only to Lk. 10:18 but also to Rev. 12:8–12.[12] In the former passage, where the Lukan Jesus responds positively to a report by seventy-two of his disciples about their recent successes in exorcistic healing (Lk. 10:17), he interprets their achievements as corresponding to the content of a visionary experience he claims to have had during the disciples' just-reported exorcistic activities: namely, he 'was seeing Satan fall like lightning from heaven' (10:18), with strong undercurrents of downward directionality being evident in the use of the verb πίπτω (aorist πεσόντα, 'fall') and reinforced by the prior description of the demons as 'submitting' (ὑποτάσσεται, 'placing themselves below or under', v. 17) to the disciples. Similarly in Rev. 12:8–12, the satanic dragon is pictured as having been thrown (ἐβλήθη, vv. 9–10) from heaven to the earth, with the implicitly downward directionality of the throwing in that context made explicit in the immediately ensuing woe addressed to the land and the sea: 'the devil has come down [κατέβη] to you' (v. 12).[13]

What makes the foregoing observations about the semantics of orientational metaphors – that is, concepts of 'up' and 'down' where nuances of success/failure, or victory/defeat, can be seen as metaphorical extensions of the strictly literal meaning of the physical directions – significant for the present inquiry is that, in addition to recurring in both the Lukan and the Revelation passages, this type of metaphor is not present in our best manuscript evidence for the Greek text of John 12:31. To be sure, in the very next clause following 12:31, the Johannine Jesus' use of the verb ὑψωθῶ (12:32) – in his anticipation of being 'lifted up' from the earth on a cross – is a heavily freighted orientational metaphor of vertical motion; but since the key clause in 12:31 about the ruler has no metaphor of vertical motion in the opposite direction, the concept in v. 32 of Jesus being lifted up derives none of its rich significance by way of contrast to v. 31b. Instead, the contrast signalled by κἀγώ[14] at the beginning of v. 32 consists of the stark differences between Jesus and the ruler, and between the increase in distance implied by being 'cast out' and the decrease in distance implied by people being drawn to Jesus.[15]

This understanding of the connection between John 12:31b and 12:32, moreover, calls for a critical rethinking of published scholarly opinion on the relationship between the envisioned expulsion of the ruler on the one hand, and the lifting up of Jesus in the crucifixion on the other hand. In brief, since the expulsion of the ruler in John 13:30 is presented in the Gospel narrative as chronologically prior to the cross event, neither the expulsion of Judas and the ruler nor the judgement it instantiates (i.e., 'the judgement of this world', John 12:31) should be understood as accomplished by Jesus' death.[16] Indeed, since Judas' withdrawal from the group has the character of a necessary condition for his subsequent self-alignment with the agents of Jesus' arrest (John 18:3–5), much better sense is made of the temporal and causal relations between the key events by construing the expulsion in 13:30 as one of several determining factors – perhaps even the most determinative of all – in the complex of happenings that culminate in the cross.[17] But just as important for my present purposes, the prominence of verticality metaphors in both Lk. 10:17–20 and Rev. 12:8–12 should now be understood as making those passages at least as significant by way of contrast to John 12:31 as by similarity to it.

Lakoff and Johnson's theorising about conceptual metaphor therefore possesses considerable power to refine our interpretation not only of important concepts in our main primary source but also of ancient comparative sources whose similarities to John 12:31 have often been exaggerated by ignoring significant ideational differences. But conceptual metaphor theory can do much more than that for the present analysis, and one of the ways in which it can help is by illuminating both how and to what degree the metaphors used in the Fourth Gospel's clause about the ruler cohere with other thematically relevant units of discourse in the Fourth Gospel.

For instance, in contrast to the particular verb forms used repeatedly in Rev. 12:9–10 to conceptualise the downfall of the devil,[18] the verb employed in John 12.31b (ἐκβληθήσεται) is a future passive of the compound form ἐκβάλλω and, as a result of its prepositional prefix, conceptualises the action as involving a container and thus also a boundary, nuances that are strengthened by the occurrence of the cognate adverb ἔξω ('out') as the next word in the same clause. The resultant concept, in the context of John 12.31, is that of an object (the 'ruler') inside a container being forcefully moved through space so as to cross a boundary which marks off the area inside the container from that outside of it, the immediate goal or end of the process being the ruler's change of location from 'in' to 'out'.[19] The predicted expulsion of the ruler in John 12:31, therefore, derives much of its meaning from the container implied by the key clause, whose in/out orientation actualises an image schema very different from the up/down orientation highlighted in Luke 10 and Revelation 12.

Despite the differences between container and verticality metaphors, both types can and often do co-occur in a single unit of discourse; and wherever they are seen to co-occur, a practitioner of critical discourse analysis may wish to read the co-occurrence as an invitation to explore, measure, and assess the relative degree of metaphorical consistency and coherence in the given piece of discourse.[20] From the methodological perspectives of both conceptual metaphor theory and critical discourse analysis, therefore, interpreters of John 12:31 ought to be analysing not only the similarities and differences between the container metaphor in our key clause and relevant concepts in the comparative sources but also the extent to which that same container metaphor might cohere with discourse elsewhere in the Fourth Gospel. For in addition to demonstrating an important aspect of good discourse analytic practice, probing the relationship between John 12:31 and its wider narrative co-text in terms of metaphorical coherence may be able to help us identify both the metaphorical container from which the Johannine 'ruler of this world' is to be expelled and thus also where and when the expulsion is to take place.

The Metaphorical Coherence of Johannine Demonology

With the expulsion of the ruler being conceptualised in John 12:31 as a forceful removal of an object from inside an assumed container to its outside, and since the phrase denoting the ruler in that context is understood by most exegetes as at least including reference to the devil,[21] the question just introduced regarding metaphorical coherence can now be explored by focusing on the ways in which space is conceptualised wherever the devil or similar entities are envisaged elsewhere in the Fourth Gospel.

In the Gospel's first reference to a diabolical being, Jesus is portrayed as responding to an expression of faith on the part of Peter by disclosing that an unnamed member of their immediate circle is διάβολος (6:70). The anarthrous state of the noun in this context has been construed by many interpreters as suggesting an indefinite nuance ('a devil').[22] But since the publication of E. C. Colwell's study of the Greek article in 1933, grammarians have increasingly highlighted the potential of anarthrous nouns to convey either a qualitative or a definite sense, with word order and other features of the given context being determinative for interpretation.[23] In the context of John 6:70, several factors converge to give διάβολος an individualising/definite nuance (i.e., 'the devil').[24] Judas, identified by name in the next verse, is therefore characterised in this context not merely as 'a devil' but rather as 'the devil', a predication that has no overtones of verticality but instead identifies Judas very closely with the devil in terms of location, attitude, and aims as an opponent of Jesus.[25]

But almost as importantly, in the narrative order of John's Gospel the first reference to the devil – or indeed to any evil spirit agency mentioned in John – is collocated in the same unit of discourse with the Fourth Gospel's initial references to Judas. With Judas and the devil thus being introduced together, in the same space both referentially and in terms of textual organisation, the closeness of the relationship between the two characters is given a high measure of prominence by means of the correspondence between the ideational and textual functions of the language used in the unit. The portrayal of the relationship between the same two characters should therefore hold no small interest to careful readers of the Gospel.

A few features of the immediate co-text of the references to Judas and the devil in 6:70–71 are worth highlighting before turning attention to other key units in the Fourth Gospel. First, although Judas is characterised twice in this context in terms of his future act of betrayal (6:64, 71), the very futurity of the betrayal as an event in the plot of the Gospel's narrative has potential to raise a question about the characterisation of Judas at the end of John 6: namely, what hints if any are present in the co-text of 6:70–71 that could shed light on what Judas may have done – or failed to do – prior to Jesus' reference to him as the devil (6:70), that could explain his being portrayed in such a fashion?

Strong hints are indeed given in the content, structure, and sequencing of the clauses constituting John 6:64, where the first of two references in this context to the betrayer (ὁ παραδώσων αὐτόν) is made by the Gospel's narrator. But first, at the beginning of that same verse, in a response by Jesus to complaints by some of his disciples about his bread-of-life discourse, he says to them: 'There are some among you who do not believe.' Immediately after that follows a more specific comment by the narrator explaining the prior statement by Jesus as grounded in his knowledge of two closely related facts: 'For Jesus knew from the beginning who were the ones that did not believe, and who was the one that would betray him' (6:64b). Both the function of that comment as an explanation of Jesus' prior utterance about the presence of unbelievers among the disciples, and the syntactical parallelism of the two clauses specifying what Jesus knew, entails that the narrator's reference to the betrayer at the end of this complex does not instantiate a separate ontological category outside that of the unbelievers mentioned in the preceding line but rather serves to highlight a particular member of the same group.

One essential part of what the Johannine Judas does to provoke Jesus' demonising degradation of his person, therefore, is to respond to Jesus in a manner void of faith or trust. But since other disciples are described in the same context as likewise lacking the desired faith, Judas' singular distinction of being the only disciple labelled in John as 'the devil'[26] cannot be explained as solely the result of his unbelief. At least one additional condition is required, and a sufficient one is implied in 6:66–71. Unlike those disciples whose interest in Jesus reached its end in their taking offence at his bread-of-life discourse (v. 60) and who distanced themselves from him accordingly (v. 66), the Johannine Judas does not withdraw from Jesus at that point but instead stays on as a member of the chosen twelve (vv. 70–71) and tacitly allows himself to be misperceived by Peter (and presumably also by the rest of the twelve) as a partner in their loyalty to Jesus (vv. 68–69).

From the details just summarised, and regardless of what the Fourth Gospel's earliest audiences may have known about Judas from other memories circulating at the time, they could easily have inferred that his behaviour towards Jesus had been deceitful and blameworthy. And shortly afterwards, where Jesus is cited as telling a group of Judean interlocutors that the devil, identified by Jesus in this context as his challengers' father, is a liar and a murderer who does not stand in the truth (8:44), a high measure of coherence can be seen between the characterisation of the devil in that context and the prior image of Judas that emerges back in 6:60–71.[27] The co-occurrence of unbelief, deceitfulness, the devil, and his murderous designs on Jesus in both 6:66–71 and 8:39–44 is reinforced by the horizontality of the Johannine presentation of the devil in both passages.

One other complex of motifs in the immediate co-text of the Judas material in John 6:60–71 has special significance for the present argument and will re-enter near its end with dramatic effect. The complex in question, although it is only present implicitly in 6:60–71, is nonetheless essential to the discourse meaning of those verses and occupies a prominent position in the frame constructed in John 6:1–59. The beginning of its development is hinted at in v. 4, where the Gospel's narrator gives his audience a meaningful note of temporal orientation for understanding the actions that follow: 'Now the Passover', he says, 'the feast-day of the Judeans, was near' (trans. mine).[28] For purposes of the present analysis, the field of discourse introduced by those words is easily ascertained by noticing the conspicuous collocation in 6:4–59 of lexemes such as ἄρτος ('bread'), φαγεῖν ('to eat'), κρίθινος ('barley'), ὀψάριον ('fish'), εὐχαριστέω ('give thanks'), κλάσματα ('fragments'), ἐμπίμπλημι ('to fill'), βρῶσις ('food'), μάννα ('manna'), πεινῶ ('be hungry'), διψω ('be thirsty'), ἀληθής πόσις ('true drink'), and τρώγω ('chew').[29] Belonging as they do to the single experiential field of meals and eating, the recurrence of this vocabulary throughout most of John 6:1–59 contributes a strong sense of focus to the narrative, plays a key role in the construction of the frame within which Judas' characterisation as a singularly diabolical unbeliever is to be understood, and thereby establishes connections between Judas, the devil, and the Jesus' circle's experiences of sharing bread and meals with each other. In diverse ways those same connections will be strengthened later in the Gospel, especially in the meal events narrated in John 12:1–8 and 13:1–30, and will play an important role below in my argument for understanding the departure of Judas in John 13:30–31 as the fulfilment of Jesus' prior word about the expulsion of the satanic ruler in 12:31b. Regarding the portrayal of Judas solely within John 6:1–59, however, it is sufficient here to note that the Gospel's first reference to Judas' diabolical unbelief is tightly interwoven both with a remarkable meal facilitated by Jesus (6:1–15), and with Judas' implied difficulties in digesting Jesus' teaching about his flesh and blood as 'true food' and 'true drink' (6:55).

Judas, however, is not mentioned in Jesus' dialogue with the Judeans in John 8, though it is certainly possible that the author of the Fourth Gospel intends his audience to recognise the family-resemblance between the Judas figure of John 6 and the Judean antagonists of Jesus in John 8.[30] Moreover, when Judas next re-enters John's narrative after his appearance in chapter 6, neither the devil nor any other evil spirit-being is mentioned in connection with him. Judas' re-entry is located textually in the story of Jesus' visit with Mary, Martha, and the recently resurrected Lazarus in Bethany (12:1–8), the nearness of another Passover of the Judeans (11:55; 12:1) being noted by the narrator as orientation for the ensuing action. As in John 6 so also in the present episode, the reference to Passover co-occurs with complicating actions that take place during a meal – in this instance, a dinner given by the hosts for Jesus. By this point in the larger narrative and in various ways, all three members of the host family have demonstrated their trust in Jesus,[31] a reality illustrated afresh in 12:3 by Mary's actions of anointing Jesus' feet with expensive perfume and wiping them with her hair. Consequently, when Judas – identified by the narrator yet again, as in 6:64–71, both as 'one of the disciples' and as 'the one about to betray' Jesus (12:4) – queries why the perfume lavished on Jesus was not sold instead for three hundred denarii so that the proceeds could be given to the poor (12:5), the contrast between Judas and the hosting party in terms of their respective dispositions to Jesus emerges clearly into the foreground of the episode. Yet the negative appraisal of Judas becomes even more salient in the next verse, where the narrator of the Gospel explains that the reason for Judas' grumble about the perfume was not any genuine concern for the poor but rather a habit of stealing from the group purse (12:6).

Implicitly at certain points but nonetheless unmistakeably, Judas therefore emerges from the comparison with Mary, Martha, and Lazarus in John 12:1–8 and its antecedent co-text (especially 8:39–47) as a faithless, traitorous, thieving liar.[32] While the story of the dinner in John 12:1–8 includes no explicit note about the diabolical essence of Judas identity, the audience of the Gospel knows more than enough about the devil by this point in the narrative to be able to infer his presence in Judas without the devil even being mentioned. Amongst named characters in the Fourth Gospel, Judas has by far the closest relationship with the devil, an affiliation described both more explicitly and as becoming more intimate in the sequence of events narrated in John 13:1–30. In that context, and as detailed below, the narration of the footwashing and related events is tied very strongly to the meal story in 12:1–8.[33]

Judas at Table

The connection between the meal episodes in John 12:1–8 and 13:1–30 consists of a number of lexical strings and reference chains which have potential to prompt the Gospel's audience to infer that Judas' eventual withdrawal from the Jesus circle (13:30) constitutes a fulfilment of Jesus' prediction in 12:31b about the expulsion of the ruler. The threads connecting the dinner stories can be summarised as follows:

1 Of the only three occurrences of the verb ἐκμάσσω ('wipe') in the Fourth Gospel, two are used to refer to Mary's wiping of Jesus' feet with her hair (11:2; 12:3), and the third is employed in John 13:5 to denote Jesus' wiping of the disciples' feet in the context of the footwashing and dinner.
2 Of the fourteen occurrences of the noun πούς ('foot') in John, eight are found in the meal-footwashing account,[34] with four of the remaining six representing actions performed by Mary relative to Jesus' feet, two of those being located in the meal story of 12:1–8 and another (11:2) being anticipatory of that episode.
3 The two episodes share an identical collocation of three lexemes relating to the temporal setting given for each story respectively: namely, the Passover (πάσχα) is mentioned explicitly at the outset (12:1; 13:1); the shared dinner (δεῖπνον) is mentioned shortly afterwards (12:2; 13:2); and the verb ἀνάκειμαι is used in the immediate co-text (12:2; 13: 23, 28) with the general sense of eating a meal, but with

additional connotations of special honour for the individual diners singled out in 12:2 (Lazarus) and 13:23 (the beloved disciple).[35]

4 Another collocational blend present in both meal episodes revolves around the presence of Judas and includes (a) his identity not only as a disciple but also as 'the betrayer';[36] (b) the disputed concern on his part about 'the poor' (12:5–8; 13:29); (c) his thieving interest in the common purse (12:6; 13:29); and (d) the prefigurative hints of his involvement in the death of Jesus.[37]

In terms of the relationship between John 12:31 and 13:30, however, the most significant link between the meal episodes in chapters 12 and 13 is yet to be mentioned.

The link in question is not lexemic in nature but largely conceptual and consists of a single command addressed in both settings by Jesus to Judas. More specifically, in John 12:7, and thus immediately after Judas' criticism of Mary regarding her use of the perfume, the first clause of Jesus' response is the command ἄφες αὐτήν ('Get away from her!'). Significantly, the verb ἀφίημι is sometimes used in the Synoptics to denote the departure of impure spirits in broadly exorcistic or other demonological discourse;[38] and when we recall that, prior to John 12:7, Judas has already been characterised in the Gospel as 'the devil' (6:70) and thus, implicitly, as exemplifying a strong family-resemblance to the Evil One (8:39–47), we have sufficient reason for reading Jesus' command to Judas in 12:7 as broadly exorcistic or at least apotropaic in register.

Consequently, when the complicating actions in the second meal scene reach a point where Jesus views Judas as needing to be addressed yet again, and with the latter now being explicitly conceptualised as a container for Satan (13:27), the sole command uttered by Jesus to Judas – 'Do quickly what you are going to do' (ὃ ποιεῖς ποίησον τάχιον) – has even stronger associations with exorcistic modes of discourse than his command back in 12:7 has; for as indicated by the connective οὖν ('therefore') in 13:30, with its familiar inferential sense,[39] followed straightaway by the narration of Judas' response to Jesus command – 'So ... he immediately went out'[40] – the satanically possessed Judas is portrayed here as understanding Jesus' command perfectly well to be a directive to get out and leave the group.

Before considering other factors bearing on the proposed connection between John 12:31 and 13:30, it should be acknowledged that none of the individual links between the meal scenes in chapters 12 and 13 possesses great strength on its own. The merit of the case for a robust linkage between the two episodes resides in the several constituent links considered together as a shared collocational set. Viewed in that fashion, the bond between the two units is strong and should not be overlooked, as indeed it often is.[41] But most significantly for the present analysis, by helping the commands of Jesus in 12:7 and 13:27 to be recognised as connoting broadly exorcistic strategies against an agent of the devil, the linkage just suggested between the meal stories in John 12–13 reinforces the impression that the relocation of Judas in 13:30 constitutes a fulfilment of the prediction back in 12:31 about the expulsion of the ruler.

To this point in the present analysis, however, my case for the prophecy-fulfilment scheme in John 12:31 and 13:30 could be assessed as only strongly suggestive. A question worth raising here, then, is what other evidence if any can be offered in support of it.

One line of support has to do with the register suggested in 12:31b by the collocation of the verb ἐκβάλλω and, with its strong potential for satanological overtones, ὁ ἄρχων τοῦ κόσμου τούτου in the brief space of the same clause. Especially if the noun phrase is assigned more or less the same referent as the Synoptic phrase ὁ ἄρχων τῶν δαιμονίων,[42] the combination sounds very much like an echo of Synoptic traditions pertaining to exorcism;[43] and while there is no need here to downplay the formal distance between the brief utterance by Jesus in John 12:31 and the lengthier stories and dialogues about exorcism in the Synoptics, the impression that the utterance in 12:31 about the ruler stands closer than any other part of the Fourth Gospel does to the conceptual world of Jesus' exorcisms in the Synoptics – especially the Beelzebul Controversy in its Lukan instantiation (Lk. 11:14–23) – has particular significance for the present inquiry. Most notably, in addition to sharing the Johannine and Matthean interests in the exorcistic process of 'casting out' (ἐκβάλλειν), the satanic 'ruler' (ὁ ἄρχων), and the keynote of judgement/judges (κρίσις/ κριτής),[44] the Lukan version allows space for the foregrounding of an exorcistic motif entirely absent from the Matthean parallel but present in John's ensuing development of the relationship between Judas and the ruler. The motif in question, present at the beginning of the Lukan account and used repeatedly in the saying directly afterwards, frames the exorcistic process not in terms of what the exorcist does but rather with reference to the demon's response: namely, the demon 'goes out' (ἐξελθόντος, Lk 11:14), a process signified not only in the Beelzebul Controversy but in several other Synoptic contexts by the use of one form or another of ἐξέρχομαι with demonic actor as grammatical subject.[45]

From the foregoing observations, a pathway to new interpretative possibilities can be cleared by asking where, following Jesus' word about the ruler in John 12:31, the ruler is described as actually vacating his container, whatever the precise nature of the latter may be. An answer worth considering in that connection comes within reach when, after he takes the morsel and becomes possessed by Satan (13:27), Judas' embodiment of Satan is understood as continuing throughout the reference chain that links Jesus' word about the coming of the ruler (14:30), the saying about the ruler having now been condemned (16:11), and Judas' arrival with soldiers for Jesus' arrest (18:3);[46] for in none of those contexts is the ruler ever portrayed as being located outside the area constituted by the body of Judas, his metaphorical container. Accordingly, wherever the Johannine Judas goes, the ruler also goes;[47] and in John 13:30, the Johannine Judas takes leave of the Jesus circle and, just like an effectively exorcised demon, goes out.

But if the interpretation suggested thus far is valid, why is it considered by so few interpreters even to be a possibility? Of the several reasons one could proffer, two possess noteworthy measures of explanatory power. First, and perhaps because the immediate co-text of the Johannine Jesus' prediction of the expulsion lacks certain features found in Synoptic and other ancient exorcism stories (e.g., reference to an individual patient), the key clauses in and around John 12:31 lack the familiar narration of the defeated spirit's departure, a motif that can only be inferred later, after an intervening stretch of text showing no interest in exorcism (i.e., John 12:32–13:25). In that light, an unsympathetic critic may wish to dismiss the present hypothesis as entailing an undesirably high degree of compositional clumsiness on the part of the ancient author; but that criticism would stand up only if we assume that John 12–13 was intended to include a conventional exorcism story like those included in the Synoptic Gospels, an assumption contravened by the form of the verb ἐκβάλλω placed on the lips of Jesus in 12:31. With the verb in that context being neither present nor aorist in form – the two most frequently used tense-forms of ἐκβάλλω in the New Testament – but rather the future form ἐκβληθήσεται, the register of the given discourse has less in common with a conventional story of exorcism in the narrow sense than with a prophecy-fulfilment scheme whose climax is initially framed not as having happened in the past but rather as still in the future from the perspective of the speaker.[48]

Additionally, because the subsequent exorcistic actions of Jesus – his giving of the morsel (13:25–26) and his word of command 'Do quickly ... ' (13:27) – are separated from the narration of Judas' departure (13:30) by the interposed note about the other disciples' misunderstanding of Jesus' directive (13:28–29), the correspondence between the exorcistic goal of Jesus and the withdrawal of Judas from the group is not so direct as to be unmistakeable. To be sure, when the aside in vv. 28–29 is read as it should be as parenthetical, the force of οὖν at the beginning of v. 30 will be taken as it is by most commentators to be introducing the result of Jesus' command and Judas' reception of the morsel: that is, Judas goes out (v. 30) because of Jesus' preceding actions of giving the morsel and the command (vv. 25–27). However, because the indirectness and consequent ambiguity in the relationship between 12:31 and 13:27–30 prevent most readers from interpreting Judas' nocturnal exit as a fulfilment of the prediction about the ruler's expulsion, the logic implicit in this part of the Johannine narrative will remain opaque unless it is explicated with the utmost care. For that purpose, Lakoff and Johnson's discussion of the logic of metaphorical containers can prove illuminating.[49]

The Logic of Containers

One of the most fundamental insights of container logic is that if object A is inside container B, and container B is inside container C, then object A must also be inside container C.[50] That basic insight acquires special value for understanding the portrayal of the satanic ruler-figure and Judas after Satan is characterised in John 13:27 as entering into Judas; for from the moment of Satan's entry into Judas until the end of John's story, the reader/audience is given no reason to assume that the location of Satan (object A) is anywhere other than inside Judas (container B), whose subsequent exit is narrated in a manner suggesting that he too has been inside a container up to that point – let us label it container C – the metaphorical container out of which Judas, and thus now also the satanic ruler inside him, are soon to be expunged. But just as importantly, and according to the same logic of containers, if container B (Judas) comes to be relocated outside of unspecified container C, object A (Satan) likewise comes to be relocated outside of C; thus, in terms of the container metaphors in the Fourth Gospel, the relocation of Judas outside of his implicit container in John 13:30 entails that the satanic ruler embodied by Judas is likewise relocated. Hence the exit of Judas in 13:30, especially since it is framed as a response to broadly exorcistic actions by Jesus (John 13:25–27), has outstanding potential to be construed as the expulsion predicted by Jesus in John 12:31.[51]

In addition to clarifying the container logic assumed in this part of the Fourth Gospel, the foregoing analysis facilitates a helpful reframing of the question raised above regarding the nature and identity of unspecified container C, the implicit container out of which the ruler in John 12:31 is eventually to be driven. Although the presence of container C in John 12:31 is too shadowy for its precise nature to be determined at that point in the narrative, information given subsequently between Jesus' prediction in that context and its fulfilment in the departure of Judas (13:30) facilitates a clearer and more confident identification; for in light of the strongly collectivist portrayal of Jesus and the disciples in 13:1–30,[52] and with any thought of the ruler's expulsion from the body of an individual human being evidently at odds with the assumptions of this particular Gospel,[53] the metaphorical container out of which the ruler is to be evicted is best understood as collective in nature. More particularly, and as Thüsing rightly intuited, both the diabolical ruler and the human host he inhabits are to be driven out of the little community of disciples.[54]

Unlike Thüsing, however, the present writer considers the proposal just sketched to possess wider interpretative consequences that heighten its significance and thus deserve fuller elaboration. For instance, since Judas is implied by Jesus and the narrator in John 13:10–11 to be polluted by a pervasive type of uncleanness that cannot be removed by footwashing,[55] his physical presence in a circle of believing disciples compromises the purity of the whole group and has potential to contaminate other members.[56] The precise nature of Judas' impurity is never made explicit in the Fourth Gospel, whose assumptions about purity more generally differ from those of the Synoptists in ways that cannot be treated in detail here;[57] but given the strong emphasis in John 6:60–71 on unbelief as an attribute of certain disciples closely associated with Judas and described as eventually withdrawing from Jesus, a disposition of unbelief towards Jesus and his words probably stands at the centre of John's concept of impurity.[58] Thus, in addition to fulfilling Jesus' prophetic word in John 12:31b about the expulsion of the ruler, the actions culminating in Judas' withdrawal from the group in 13:30 constitute both a process of purification – Judas, as the in-group unbeliever, the enemy within, is now relocated and at last put in his proper place, outside the community of the faithful – and a ritual paradigm whereby protection against 'the evil one' (τοῦ πονηροῦ, 17:15) can be accessed by Jesus' followers in the days ahead;[59] for as implied in both the footwashing instruction (13:1–20) and Jesus' discourse on the vineyard and the vines (15:1–8), the single instance of cleansing and protection effected by the expulsion in John 13:30 is not intended to afford by itself the same benefits for Christ associations in post-Easter settings but instead is presented as a model for group re-enactment in those later contexts.[60]

As in the Synoptics, therefore, so also in John 13 a subtle blending of demonological discourse and the semantics of purity/impurity is apparent, an interface given further attention below. But just as importantly, the potential of the narration of Judas' withdrawal in John 13:30 to be interpreted as the climax of a purification event is realised in part by the presence and sequencing of two container metaphors in 13:27–30 which cohere with that treated above in connection with 12:31. First, in 13:27 the narration of Satan's taking possession of Judas immediately after the footwashing episode is conceptualised in the familiar form of an individual human becoming a container inside of which a noxious spirit agency relocates itself – Judas having received the morsel, 'Satan entered into him' (εἰσῆλθεν εἰς ἐκεῖνον ὁ σατανᾶς, 13.27) – a process whose framing, like that of the expulsion anticipated back in 12:31, has no overtones of verticality. The grammatical pattern of the key clause in 13:27 – a verb with a prepositional prefix (εἰσῆλθεν) + independent use of the same preposition in a circumstantial element (εἰς ἐκεῖνον) + diabolical subject denoted by an articular substantive (ὁ σατανᾶς) – is closer than that of any other clause in the Fourth Gospel to the expulsion prophecy in 12:31.[61] The grammatical pattern instantiated in John 12:31, therefore, contributes both to the highlighting of a striking opposition between the motions of Satan/RW[62] in the key clauses of 12:31 and 13:27 – the ruler's movement *out of* a container in 12.31, Satan's movement *into* a container in 13.27[63] – and to a frequently overlooked reference chain linking the ruler in the prior clause to Satan in the latter. The link between the ruler in 12:31 and Satan in 13:27, although it is inadequate by itself to require the audience to infer the proposed prophecy-fulfilment scheme, significantly increases both the textual strength of the scheme and the merit of the proposed reading.

Furthermore, since the descriptions of the relationship between the devil and Judas in John 6:70 and 13:2 are not entirely clear in sense and do not require the Gospel's audience to assume that Judas has become diabolically possessed prior to his reception of the morsel in 13:26–27,[64] the note in 13:27 about Satan entering into Judas signals a development towards greater clarity in their relationship. The same note also helps the audience to be mindful as to where the satanic ruler is located at this precise moment in the plot, when the metaphorical container he has just entered – Judas – is about to make his own exit. However, while the note concerning Satan's entry into Judas effectively sets the stage for his withdrawal to function simultaneously as a purification of the Jesus group, it needs help to signal the purification proper. The necessary help is given in the form of the compound verb ἐξέρχομαι, essential to the second container metaphor previewed above and used twice by the narrator in John 13:30–31 to denote the process whereby Judas physically relocates himself from inside the social body of the Jesus circle to the worldly space of darkness outside that body. From the standpoint of the narrator of John 13:27–30, therefore, immediately after Satan 'went into' (εἰσῆλθεν, v. 27) Judas, Judas himself 'went out' (ἐξῆλθεν, v. 30) from the disciples, taking the satanic ruler with him. The narrator's immediate reuse of the same form of the latter verb at the beginning of v. 31 – 'So when Judas went out [ἐξῆλθεν], Jesus said, "Now the Son of Man is glorified …"' (v. 31) – directly after his brief but loaded note ἦν δὲ νύξ ('And it was night'), has the effect of increasing the salience of Judas and the satanic ruler's departure, whilst also reframing that event as temporal orientation to Jesus' ensuing utterance. Indeed, because the two occurrences of ἐξῆλθεν in these clauses tightly sandwich the intervening note about the expulsion's nocturnal timing, the whole sequence is easily construed as part of a scheme initiated back in 12.28–36; where the co-occurrence of Jesus' prophecy of expulsion (and its container metaphor, 12.31), the dense repetition of the verb δοξάζω directly beforehand (12.28), and the immediately ensuing discourse about light and darkness (12.35–36) anticipates the collocation of Judas' departure with Satan, the symbolic reference to its night-time setting, and the repetition of δοξάζω in Jesus' verbal response to Judas' withdrawal.[65]

The particular collocation and distribution of features just described contribute to the formation of a larger chiastic structure that can be outlined as follows:

A. Foregrounded discourse of glory, 12:28
B. Prediction of the ruler's expulsion, 12:31
C. Out-group unbelief as fulfilment of Isaianic prophecy, 12:34–43 (esp. vv. 37–41)
D. Footwashing as symbolic removal of dirt from the body, 13:1–17
C.* In-group unbelief (i.e., Judas) as fulfilment of prophetic words, 13:18–29
B.* Fulfilment of the expulsion prediction, 13:30
A.* Foregrounded discourse of glory, 13:31–32

By drawing attention to the multiple links between 12:28–36 and 13:27–32, the scheme just inferred strengthens the case for reading Jesus' word about the ruler in John 12:31b and the subsequent narration of Judas' withdrawal from the disciples as forming a prophecy-fulfilment structure. But just as importantly, since the third-person singular passive of δοξάζω (ἐδοξάσθη) is combined in a single clause of John 13:31 with the first occurrence of the adverb νῦν since John 12:31 – 'Now the Son of Man has been glorified' (νῦν ... ἐδοξάσθη) – that clause in particular has potential to sum up the various effects of Judas' withdrawal, its purifying significance for the community of believing disciples, and its fulfilment not only of Jesus' prophetic word in 12:31 about the expulsion but also of the promise by the heavenly voice in 12:28 to glorify yet again the name of the Father.[66]

Notes

1 Following the outline and headings proposed by Brown, *John I–XII*, p. cxxxviii.
2 See, e.g., Schnelle, *Das Evangelium nach Johannes*, 228; Beasley-Murray, *John*, 213–14; Thyen, *Das Johannes-evangelium*, 565–66.
3 Identical in 16:11 but without the adjectival pronoun in 14:30.
4 Also used in 6:70, anarthrously but with an individualising nuance as defended below.
5 Taking τοῦ πονηροῦ in 17:15 as masculine ('the evil one'), not neuter ('evil', as an abstract substantive). On the near consensus in the scholarly literature, cf. Wright and Davies, '"John, Jesus, and "the Ruler of This World"'", 75–76, 78. Barrett, *The Gospel According to St John*, 426–27, 510 is a clear example. The referential overlap recognised by Barrett and many others is partly obscured by the semantic-field analysis in J. P. Louw and E. A. Nida, *Greek-English Lexicon of the New Testament Based on Semantic Domains*, 2nd edn, vol. I (New York: United Bible Societies, 1989), 137, 145–48, who acknowledge that their distinction between 'supernatural beings' (e.g., θεός and διάβολος) and 'supernatural powers' (e.g., ἄρχων τῆς ἐξουσίας τοῦ ἀέρος) is artificial (p. 136, n. 1).

6 Wright and Davies, 'John, Jesus', and "The Ruler of This World"', 74-87.
7 On cohesive ties, parallelism, and other schematic devices as 'extra structure' that prompts for inferencing above the level of individual clauses, see R. Fowler, *Linguistic Criticism*, 2nd edn (Oxford: Oxford University Press, 1996), 92-109.
8 As implied in John 13:27 by the description Satan's possession of Judas.
9 See, e.g., Piper, 'The Absence of Exorcism', 275.
10 See, e.g., Wengst, *Das Johannes-evangelium*, II, 75-76; Schnackenburg, *The Gospel According to St John*, II, 391-92; Moloney, *Signs and Shadows*, 191-92; and Barrett, *The Gospel According to St John*, 427 ('Nothing is said of his subsequent fate'). A better sense of development is offered by W. Sproston, 'Satan in the Fourth Gospel', in *Studia Biblica 1978, II. Papers on the Gospels, Sixth International Congress on Biblical Studies, Oxford 3-7 April 1978*, ed. E. A. Livingstone (Sheffield: JSOT, 1980), 307-311, but with only cursory comment on 12:31 and 13:30, and thus without considering the possibility that the prediction in the former is presented as fulfilled in the latter.
11 As explained in Lakoff and Johnson, *Metaphors We Live By*, 14-25, orientational metaphors conceptualise experiences in terms of spatial orientation: up-down, in-out, front-back, on-off, deep-shallow, near-far etc. 'Kevin fell into a depression.' 'The speaker's presentation strayed far from the topic.'
12 See note 2 above for representative proponents.
13 Interpretations that minimise the differences between John 12:31 and comparative texts in Luke and Revelation are subjected to penetrating critique, with consequences like those embraced here, in J. Leonhardt-Balzer, 'The Ruler of the World, Antichrists and Pseudo-Prophets: Johannine Variations on an Apocalyptic Motif', in *John's Gospel and Intimations of Apocalyptic*, ed. C. H. Williams and C. Rowland (London: Bloomsbury, 2013), 183-84.
14 Crasis from καὶ ἐγώ, here 'but I'.
15 BAGD, 'κἀγώ', 386, sees a contrast ('but I ... ') strictly between Jesus and the ruler, says nothing about what the relevant difference(s) might be, and thus shows no sign of viewing up/down as part of the contrast.
16 As indeed it often is; see, e.g., Schnelle, *Das Evangelium nach Johannes*, 228; Beasley-Murray, *John*, 213-14; and J. Dennis, 'The "Lifting Up of the Son of Man" and the Dethroning of the "Ruler of This World": Jesus' Death as the Defeat of the Devil in John 12,31-32', in *The Death of Jesus in the Fourth Gospel*, ed. G. Van Belle (BETL, 200; Leuven: Peeters Leuven, 2007), 679-82, 685, 689. A strong influence on the last of those studies being the lure of identifying 'the cross event' as the moment anticipated in John 12:31, as the eschatological hour of Jesus' triumph over Satan, Dennis is led into ignoring the difference between being 'cast out' and being 'cast down' (682, 685); as a result, he is also drawn into over-specifying the temporal reference of νῦν, in John 12:31, as limited to Jesus' death (679 n. 9), instead of encompassing the larger sequence of events (including Judas' departure in John 13:30) leading up to that death. On the Johannine 'hour' of fulfilment as the larger sequence of 'divinely ordained events' from the footwashing episode to the end of the Johannine passion narrative, cf. J. C. Thomas, *Footwashing in John 13 and the Johannine Community*, 2nd edn (Cleveland, TN: CPT Press, 2014), 111.
17 On the relationship between the expulsion in John 13:30 and the cross event, strong support for the alternative proposal above exists in the perfect tense-form of κέκριται in John 16:11, where the collocation of the κρίνω/κρίσις group and ὁ ἄρχων τοῦ κόσμου τούτου contributes to a sense that 'the judgement of this world' anticipated in 12:31 is no longer seen as imminent or in the process of being realised but rather, from the temporal perspective of Jesus as

the speaker in 16:11, as now being complete. The terse comment by Thüsing on 16:11 (*Die Erhöhung und Verherrlichung Jesu*, 143), read in the light of his handling of the prediction in 12:31 (p. 22), hints at an interpretation of 16:11 similar to that suggested here but without noting the evidentiary value of the shift from κρίσις, sandwiched by νῦν and the aspectually vague ἐστιν ('Now is the condemnation', 12:31b), to the more precise blend of completive and stative nuances in the perfect tense-form κέκριται ('... has been condemned', 16:11).

18 I.e., ἐβλήθη and ἐβλήθησαν, aorist passive forms of βάλλω without either the prepositional prefix ἐκ– or the cognate adverb ἔξω in the same clause.

19 Cf. Louw and Nida, *Greek-English Lexicon*, vol. I, 723: 'extension to a goal ... outside a presumed area', as illustrated also inJohn 6:37 and Mt. 13:48.

20 A thorough introduction to metaphorical coherence and closely related concepts is provided by Lakoff and Johnson, *Metaphors We Live By*, 22–24, 41–45, and 77–105.

21 As discussed at the beginning of the present and preceding chapters.

22 See, e.g., Thyen, *Das Johannes-evangelium*, 382; Lincoln, *The Gospel According to Saint John*, 352; and many English translations (e.g., the KJV, RSV, NRSV, ASV, NIV, NKJV, and JB).

23 See E. C. Colwell, 'A Definite Rule for the Use of the Article in the Greek New Testament', *JBL* 52 (1933): 12–21, whose findings on most points have been embraced but also critically refined by D. B. Wallace, *Greek Grammar Beyond the Basics: An Exegetical Syntax of the New Testament* (Grand Rapids: Zondervan, 1996), 256–70; S. E. Porter, *Idioms of the Greek New Testament*, Biblical Languages: Greek, 2 (Sheffield: JSOT Press, 1992), 103–105; and C. F. D. Moule, *An Idiom Book of New Testament Greek*, 2nd edn (Cambridge: Cambridge University Press, 1959), 111–17.

24 Cf. G. J. Riley, 'Devil', in *Dictionary of Deities and Demons in the Bible*, ed. K. van der Toorn, B. Becking, and P. W. van der Horst (Leiden: E. J. Brill, 1995), col. 471. In the key clause of John 6:70 (καὶ ἐξ ὑμῶν εἷς διάβολος ἐστιν), the noun exemplifies all the defining features of an anarthrous pre-verbal predicate nominative, a particular type of usage whose definiteness/indefiniteness is increasingly understood as best established not from the absence of the article but rather from pertinent features of the context. The anarthrous usage of διάβολος in 1 Pet. 5:8 and Rev. 20:2 is normally understood likewise as having definite meaning ('the devil'). An indefinite nuance ('a devil') in any of these passages would entail the existence of multiple 'devils', whereas the substantival usage of διάβολος in the NT is always singular – note especially John 8:44 and 13:2 – and likewise more generally in early Jewish and Christian literature when the referent is a supramundane power (e.g., as the rendering of שטן in LXX 1 Chron. 21:1; Job 1:6 - 2:7, Zech. 3:1–3); see also WisSol 2:24; Mt. 4:1; Eph. 4:27; Heb. 2:14; Ign. *Eph.* 10:3; *Trall.* 8:1; *Rom.* 5:3; *Smyrn.* 9:1. The only NT occurrences of διάβολος in the plural (1 Tim. 3:11; 2 Tim. 3:3; and Titus 2:3) are adjectival and thus refer neither to 'the devil' nor to a demon but instead signify a negative trait attributed to human antagonists. Colwell, 'A Definite Rule', 20; Wallace, *Greek Grammar Beyond the Basics*, 257.

25 Like the relationship between Judas and 'the ruler of this world', as suggested in the present analysis; cf. Pagels, *The Origin of Satan*, 100–102, 105–106, 111.

26 Jesus' characterisation of his Judean interlocutors in John 8:44 as having the devil as their father belongs to the same broad field of satanological discourse and deviance-labeling; but the linguistic devices used in the two passages are perceptibly different, with fictive kinship being the operative concept in 8:44 but metaphorical resemblance being the idea in 6:70.

27 Cf. W. M. Wright, 'Greco-Roman Character Typing and the Presentation of Judas in the Fourth Gospel', *CBQ* 71.3 (2009): 553–56.

28 The importance of the ritual meal as part of the Passover festival is implied in the Synoptics (Mt. 26:17; Mk 14:12–22; Lk. 22:8–16). As noted by J. Unterman, 'Passover', in *Harper's Bible Dictionary*, ed. P. Achtemeier (San Francisco, HarperCollins, 1985), 753, the apotropaic function of the ritual is highlighted in Exod. 12:1–13:16, esp. 12:7–13, a feature not without relevance to the meal in John 13:1–30 according to the reading developed below. Although the meal in John 13 is not a Passover meal, the setting indicated in 13:1 loosely associates it with Passover and, as noted by Lincoln (*The Gospel According to Saint John*, 365), makes the death of Jesus in the Fourth Gospel 'coincide with the slaughter of the Passover lambs'.

29 The noun ἄρτος occurs twenty-one times in John 6:5–58; φαγεῖν fourteen times in the same section; and κρίθινος twice as a qualifier of ἄρτος (6:9, 13); all collocated with ὀψάριον (6:9, 11), εὐχαριστήσας διέδωκεν ('give thanks', 6:11, 23), κλάσματα ('fragments' of food, 6:12, 13), ἐμπίμπλημι ('be filled/satisfied' with food, 6:12), βρῶσις ('food', 6:27², 55), μάννα ('manna', 6:31, 49), πεινῶ ('have hunger', 6:35), διψῶ ('have thirst', 6:35), ἀληθής πόσις ('true drink', 6:55), and τρώγω ('chew', 6:54, 56–58).

30 Like Judas in John 6:60–71, the Judean antagonists of Jesus in John 8:34–50 are closely associated with the devil, are hostile to the truth, reject Jesus' word, and have murderous intentions towards him; cf. R. A. Culpepper, *Anatomy of the Fourth Gospel: A Study in Literary Design* (Philadelphia: Fortress, 1983), 124. At least two features in the immediate co-text of Judas' introduction in John 6:64–71 reinforce the resemblance just noted and increase the probability that it is rhetorically motivated. First, immediately after the initial mention of Judas' name in the Gospel (τὸν Ἰούδαν, 6:71), four morphemically related Greek words – two forms of Ἰουδαία ('Judea', 7:1, 3) and two of Ἰουδαῖος (Judean/Jew, 7:1, 2) – contribute to a short but dense lexical string whose inclusion of the name 'Judas' is more easily recognised in the Greek text than in many modern translations; thus, from the very first mention of Judas in the Fourth Gospel, his association with the concepts of Judea and being Judean is foregrounded. The existence of the same association is made additionally clear by the narrator's reference to Judas in 6:71 as 'the son of Simon Iscariot' – i.e., Simon from Kerioth – a reference that frames Judas' identity in terms of his father's association with a village in southern Judea. The resultant foregrounding of the relationship between Judas and all things Judean in John 6:71 – 7:3 has potential to make the connotations of the whole word-group even more negative than some Johannine scholars have allowed; see, e.g., A. Reinhartz, 'The Jews of the Fourth Gospel', in *The Oxford Handbook of Johannine Studies*, ed. J. M. Lieu and M. C. de Boer (Oxford: Oxford University Press, 2018), 123; and P. F. Esler and R. A. Piper, *Lazarus, Mary and Martha: A Social-Scientific and Theological Reading of John* (London: SCM, 2006), 161–62. The lexical string tying together John 6:71–7:3, therefore, deserves more attention than it normally receives in scholarship regarding John and anti-Judaism, a topic whose complexities defy adequate coverage here.

31 In addition to the implications of the narrator's identification of Martha, Mary, and Lazarus as particular recipients of Jesus' love (John 11:5), Martha is cited as making an exemplary confession of faith in 11:27; Mary is portrayed in 11:32 as kneeling at Jesus' feet and expressing faith in his power over death; and Lazarus, despite being dead, obeys Jesus' command to come out of the tomb (11:43–44). Cf. Culpepper, *Anatomy of the Fourth Gospel*, 142.

32 The beloved three from Bethany, in preparing the dinner for Jesus (12:2) after his resurrection of Lazarus, exemplify a blend of reciprocity, gratitude, and attachment indicative of genuine faith; and as noted by J. Neyrey, *The Gospel of John in Cultural and Rhetorical Perspective* (Grand Rapids: Eerdmans, 2009), 339, the kindness of Mary in particular exposes by contrast the dishonesty, greed, and treachery of Judas. On lying as a trait shared by the Johannine Judas (12:4–6) and the devil (8:44), in contrast to Jesus, who speaks the truth (8:45) and is the truth (14:6), see W. M. Wright, 'Greco-Roman Character Typing', 455.

33 Cf. Thyen, *Das Johannes-evangelium*, 601; and F. Moloney, *Glory not Dishonor: Reading John 13–21* (Minneapolis: Fortress, 1998), 13.

34 John 13:5, 6, 8, 9, 10, 12, 14².

35 Louw and Nida, *Greek-English Lexicon*, vol. I, 218–19, 251–52.

36 John 12:4; 13:2, 18, 21.

37 John 12:7–8; 13:1–4, 11, 18–19, 21–30.

38 See, e.g., Mt. 4:11 (par. Mk 1:31); 8:15 (par. Lk. 4:39); John 4:52; and perhaps also John 18:8. On fever as a demonic spirit of illness in Lk. 4:39 and ancient comparative sources (e.g., *4QExorcism ar*), see Klutz, *The Exorcism Stories in Luke-Acts*, 75–78. The semantic space shared by ἀφίημι and ὑπάγω in Mt. 4:10–11 entails that Jesus' command to Peter, ὕπαγε ὀπίσω μου, σατανᾶ, in Mt. 16:23 is broadly similar in force to the command in John 12:7.

39 I.e., partly as a result of taking the morsel (λαβὼν οὖν τὸ ψωμίον) but also in response to Jesus' command (v. 27), the latter being presented as closer than the former to the moment of Judas departure. On the cause(s) of Judas' withdrawal, the command by Jesus is assigned far greater weight than the morsel by Wengst, *Das Johannes-evangelium*, vol. 2, 114. On resultative οὖν, see Louw and Nida, *Greek-English Lexicon*, vol. 1, 783.

40 The adverbs τάχιον ('quickly, in a brief period of time', v. 27) and εὐθύς ('immediately', directly after some previous point in time, v. 30) are not identical in sense but, as noted by Lincoln, *The Gospel according to Saint John*, 380, serve well together in this context to portray Judas' departure in v. 30 as an immediate act of obedience to Jesus' command in v. 27. Widely overlooked, however, is the comparable emphasis on the prompt obedience of demons in response to authoritative commands or similar gestures in a range of ancient exorcistic sources; see, e.g., Tobit[S] 8:3; Mark 1:42; Acts 16:18; Josephus, *Ant.* 8.47; *PGM* 4.1242–46. The motif of prompt demonic response to the exorcistic command in Acts 16:18 is combined with repetition of ἐξέρχομαι (16:18–19) in a way that closely parallels John 13:30–31.

41 Entirely overlooked, e.g., by Bultmann, *The Gospel of John*, 457–86, perhaps partly due to affinity for redaction-critical hypotheses that take no notice of lexical strings such as those connecting Jesus' glory discourse in John 12:28 and that in 13:31 (ibid., 461); and placed so far in the background as to be nearly hidden in Barrett, *The Gospel According to Saint John*, 435–49. The connection between the two supper narratives is recognised by Martin, *Judas and the Rhetoric of Comparison*, 148, n. 42, but without considering the broadly exorcistic potential of the commands in 12:7 and 13:27.

42 I.e., as a reference to Satan; and as understood, e.g., by Brown, *John I-XII*, 468; and Bultmann, *The Gospel of John*, 431. The Synoptic phrase: Mt. 12:24 (par. Mk 3:22; Lk. 11:15).

43 On echoes of Synoptic exorcism traditions in the Fourth Gospel more generally, see Piper, 'The Absence of Exorcism', 206; E. Plumer, 'The Absence of Exorcisms in the Fourth Gospel', *Bib* 78 (1997): 350–68; E. K. Broadhead, 'Echoes of an Exorcism in the Fourth Gospel?', *ZNW* 86 (1995): 111–19; and

B. Lindars, 'Rebuking the Spirit: A New Analysis of the Lazarus Story of John 11', *NTS* 38 (1992): 89–104.
44 ἐκβάλλειν: Lk. 11:15–20[4] (par. Mt. 12:24–28[4]; John 12:31); ὁ ἄρχων: Lk. 11:15 (par. Mt. 12:24; John 12:31); and κρίσις/κριτής: Lk. 11:19 (par. Mt. 12:27; John 12:31).
45 Mt. 8:32 (par. Mk 5:13; Lk. 8:33); 12:43–44 (par. Lk. 11:24²); 17:18 (par. Mk 9:26); Mk 1:26 (par. Lk. 4:35); 7:29–30; 9:29; Lk. 4:36, 41; 8:2, 35, 38; 11:14. See also Acts 8:7; 16:18–19. The verb ἐξέρχομαι is used in various types of contexts and with a wide range of grammatical subjects, so it is not to be seen as a technical term for exorcistic processes; instead, the point to be inferred from the preceding list of references is that the employment of ἐξέρχομαι to denote the departure of demons from their hosts is attested in several Synoptic contexts some of which were probably known to the author of the Fourth Gospel.
46 As noted with admirable clarity by Schnelle, *Das Evangelium nach Johannes*, 261, 287, the coming of Judas' against Jesus in John 18:3 is presented as, *inter alia*, a fulfilment of Jesus' prophetic comment in 14:30 that 'the ruler is coming', a reference to the diabolical figure whose presence and influence in the Fourth Gospel are mediated at several junctures by Judas; and the connection between those two references confirms that the same two figures must be in view yet again when Jesus pronounces in 16:11 that, 'regarding condemnation, the ruler of this world has been condemned' (i.e., in the eviction of Judas back in 13:30). But most importantly, with the coming of the ruler in 14:30 entailing that he is not physically present among the disciples at the time of Jesus' utterance in that context, and the condemnation of the ruler in 16:11 not being 'now' or imminent (as it is in 12:31) but rather already enacted (perfect tense κέκριται with stative aspect, 16:11), the spatiotemporal point of view attributed to Jesus in 14:30 and 16:11 has changed from that assumed in 12:31; and the best explanation of that change is that the condemnation by expulsion, anticipated as imminent in 12:31, is conceptualised as having been achieved by the time of Jesus' utterances in 14:30 and 16:11.
47 Cf. Sproston, 'Satan in the Fourth Gospel', 309: 'For the fourth evangelist the presence of Judas is synonymous with the presence of the devil.'
48 Of the verb's seventy-six occurrences in the NT, only two are in the future – John 12:31 and Mt. 8:12 – with forty-three in the aorist, thirty in the present, and one in the imperfect. The use of ἐκβάλλω with the adverb ἔξω in John 9:34–35 ('And they drove him out', v. 34) to describe the Judean opponents' expulsion of the man healed of blindness, especially in a context of concern about Christ-followers being excluded from the local synagogue (9:22), represents a situation similar to that inferred from the proposed scheme involving Judas and the ruler in 12:31 and 13:30; but just as importantly, the same pattern of usage also reinforces the impression that the metaphorical containers out of which deviant persons in the given context are expelled have strong potential to be social or group-oriented in nature.
49 Lakoff and Johnson, *Philosophy in the Flesh*, 380–82, 544–45.
50 As Lakoff and Johnson (*Philosophy in the Flesh*, 380–82) emphasise, the classic formulation of 'container logic' just summarised comes to us from Aristotle and the system of formal logic on which his theories of classification, categories, knowledge of causes, and scientific explanation are based. From the perspective of Lakoff and Johnson's own variety of cognitive science, however, Aristotle's logic of containers is best understood as a frequently apt conceptual metaphor – namely, the metaphor 'Categories Are Containers' (i.e., bounded regions in space) – but not, as Aristotle himself assumed, a consistently reliable method of acquiring knowledge of the essences of things in the world.

51 I.e., as the climax of an exorcistic event, broadly conceived. The potential for that effect is increased by a feature not yet mentioned above (or elsewhere, to my knowledge): namely, the combination of morphological repetition and antonymy in the co-occurrence of εἰσῆλθεν (Satan's entry, 13:27) and ἐξῆλθεν (the possessed Judas' exit, 13:30–31) within the same unit of discourse, in conjunction with the semantic field of evil supramundane beings (e.g., Satan, 13:27); a pattern of discourse likewise exemplified in the Lukan version of Jesus' exorcistic healing of the man from Gerasa (Lk. 8:26–39; par. Mt. 8:28–34; Mk 5:1–20) – a version that may have been familiar to the author of the Fourth Gospel – with the Lukan account's three occurrences of εἰσέρχομαι, four occurrences of ἐξέρχομαι, and legion of demons. On the Lukan account and its own distinctive emphases, see Klutz, *The Exorcism Stories in Luke-Acts*, 82–151.

52 In this section of the Gospel the disciples as a distinct group are either referred to or implicitly envisaged repeatedly through the use of plural pronouns (e.g., 13:1, 10, 14, 18–21, 22), plural nouns (e.g., 13:5, 23), and plural verb forms (13:12–15, 17, 29).

53 Out of the question, i.e., because the author of the Fourth Gospel apparently has reservations about exorcism in the narrow sense, and even though he can be seen to broaden the category for his own purposes in John 12:31 and 13:27–30. On the reservations, again see Piper, 'The Absence of Exorcism', 253–78, and the literature cited there.

54 Thüsing, *Die Erhöhung und Verherrlichung Jesu*, 22 n. 43. Leonhardt-Balzer, 'The Ruler of the World, Antichrists, and Pseudo-Prophets', in Williams and Rowland (ed.), *John's Gospel and Intimations of Apocalyptic*, 186–87, leans towards a partly similar interpretation by reading the prediction in John 12:31 as anticipating the expulsion of the ruler, not from the world, but rather 'from the community'; but unlike Thüsing and the present analysis, her study shows no interest in the possibility of reading that same prediction as contributing to a prophecy-fulfilment scheme with the narration of Judas' departure in John 13:30 at its end.

55 Or, for that matter, by what the footwashing symbolises: namely, and as discussed in the next two chapters, the larger and more complex process – culminating in John 13:30 – of expunging the Johannine Judas from the social body of the Jesus circle; but as part of that same process, perhaps also the eucharist (cf. Martin, *Judas and the Rhetoric of Comparison*, 148), with particular reference to its destructive potential for those who receive it unworthily (see, e.g., 1 Cor. 11:27–32).

56 Cf. 1 Cor. 5:6, 'A little yeast leavens the whole batch of dough'.

57 On purity in the Fourth Gospel, and more particularly in John 13, see T. Kazen, *Jesus and Purity Halakhah: Was Jesus Indifferent to Impurity* (CB; Stockholm: Almqvist & Wiksell, 2002), 248–55, who, despite focusing largely on what can be learned from John about the historical Jesus and his Second Temple Jewish context, has a view of the Gospel's own perspective similar to that proposed above.

58 For the purity discourse in John 13:10–11, a suggestion similar to that above is made by E. Kobel, *Dining with John: Communal Meals and Identity Formation in the Fourth Gospel and its Historical and Cultural Context* (Biblical Interpretaton 109; Leiden: Brill, 2011), 204, who rightly observes that the explanation by the narrator in John 13:10–11 ('For he knew who was to betray him; for this reason he said, "Not all of you are clean"', NRSV) implies that betrayal is 'an act of impurity'; however, when that same passage is read in the light of both the portrayal of Judas in John 6:64–71 and the

conceptualisation of purification in 15:1–8, the phenomenon of betrayal acquires strong potential to be seen as an outworking of unbelief, whose presence inside the Jesus circle entails the accompaniment of impurity as the author of John's Gospel (re)defines it.

59 On τοῦ πονηροῦ as masculine and personal ('the evil one') rather than neuter and abstract ('evil'), and thus as co-referential with ὁ ἄρχων τοῦ κόσμου, see L. T. Stuckenbruck, 'Evil in Johannine and Apocalyptic Perspective: Petition for Protection in John 17', in Williams and Rowland (ed.), *John's Gospel and Intimations of Apocalyptic*, 202–204. In addition to clarifying that the protection mentioned by Jesus in John 17:12 should be identified with Jesus' removal of Judas from the group in 13:26–30, the reading proposed in the present study suggests an answer to Stuckenbruck's question (p. 204) concerning why, after claiming to 'have conquered the world' (16:33), the Johannine Jesus finds it necessary to pray that his followers be protected from 'the evil one' (17:15). As will become clearer in the next chapter, while the protection of Jesus' followers must be modelled upon the paradigm of association order demonstrated in Jesus' ousting of Judas, the actualisation of their protection in the post-Easter world of Christian assemblies will require a synergetic co-operation of those assemblies with the Father whom Jesus petitions.

60 The interpretation outlined above for the footwashing episode has attractive implications for how the practice of this custom might have been expected to function in the ancient setting of Christ-group meals: namely, the members' washing of one another's feet would serve as a powerful reminder that, just as literal dirt is removed from a part of the individual human body through footwashing, so also the religious/spiritual 'dirt' (i.e., impurity) of unbelieving members of the Christ association must be removed from the group as a social body. Wherever the removal of unsuitable members was needed, moreover, the exclusionary potential of the eucharist and the word would have been operative – or at least they would have been assumed to be so – as in the cases of Judas in John 13:26–30 and the immoral member described in 1 Cor. 5:1–13. Overall, the model of practice inferred here agrees with Thomas, *Footwashing*, 189–91, both on the embedding of footwashing in the setting of a group meal, and on the participation of all members of the group in the performance; but takes exception to Thomas's ideas about the assumed context involving a 'Johannine community'; the suggestion that the footwashing was understood to cleanse believers from post-conversion sin; and the use of *Didache* 14 as evidence for confession of sin being part of the Johannine routine.

61 I.e., the compound verb ἐκβληθήσεται, the reoccurrence of the prefixed morpheme ἐκ in the cognate adverb ἔξω, and the articular noun phrase ὁ ἄρχων τοῦ κόσμου τούτου.

62 Because the co-referentiality of 'Satan' and 'the ruler of this world' is important to bear in mind in the remainder of the present inquiry, 'RW' will be used alongside 'the devil' or 'Satan' as shorthand for 'the ruler of this world' wherever a reminder seems advisable in the remaining pages of the present study.

63 As noted, e.g., by Thyen, *Das Johannes-evangelium*, 602, and many others, the Johannine representation of Satan's entry into Judas is similar to the account in Lk. 22:3 and may be an instance of Lukan influence on the Fourth Gospel. But whatever origins we might imagine for the Johannine clause, it plays a vital role in creating the conditions for Judas' subsequent departure (13:30) to be construed as a fulfilment of the prediction uttered by Jesus in 12:31.

64 On p. 15 nn. 22–24 above, my interpretation of διάβολος in John 6:70 as definite ('the devil') was interested only in the grammatical problem posed by

the Colwell construction (i.e., the anarthrous pre-verbal predicate nominative). But as noted by Wallace, *Greek Grammar Beyond the Basics*, 249, the construction is also metaphorical, with διάβολος being used as a familiar source domain for conceptualising Judas, as the less familiar target domain whose nature and disposition are unknown to Jesus' auditors in 6:60–71 and remain at least partly hidden from most or all of them as late as the last supper (13:21–30); the grammar and semantics of the clause in 6:70, therefore, do not entail that Judas has become satanically possessed by that early point in the plot. As for the narrator's comment about the devil in John 13:2, the most difficult of the attested variants has Judas' name in the nominative (Ἰούδας, rather than the genitive Ἰούδα), is favoured by the best Greek witnesses (p^{66}, p^{75vid}, a, B), and thus is not explicit whether the devil put the idea of betrayal into Judas' heart or instead into his own; but the active form of βάλλω (perf. βεβληκότος), attested across the Greek witnesses in conjunction with εἰς ('into'), is more consistent with the image of one personal agent getting under the skin of another than it is with a single agent acting mentally upon themselves, for which the middle form βεβλημένου would have been the natural choice. The use of καρδία in John 12:40 to refer to human hearts supports the same conclusion. In John 13:2, therefore, the devil is best understood as acting on Judas' heart from outside, a scenario that makes Satan's subsequent action of entering Judas (13:27) a new and more dramatic complication en route to the climax in 13:30. The treatment of the problem in Brown, *John XIII–XXI*, 550 includes penetrating assessment of earlier scholarly discussion (esp. Bultmann and Barrett) but underestimates the significance of whether it is Judas' heart or Satan's that is in view.

65 The most conspicuous of these links is the repetition of δοξάζω in both contexts (12:28; 13:31–32); for in addition to the high density of the repetition in both cases (3x in 12:28; 5x in 13:31–32), these are the only passages in the Fourth Gospel where the repetition of δοξάζω is accompanied by the grammatical pattern of aorist forms opening the sequence and future forms closing it. The lexical string connecting 12:28 and 13:31–32, therefore, possesses considerable strength and, in conjunction with other prominent features in the immediate co-text, creates good potential for the schematic structure outlined here to be inferred.

66 I.e., καὶ πάλιν δοξάσω, 'and I will glorify it [i.e., the name] again'.

3 Exorcism, Meal, and Morsel in John 12–13

Magic, Disenchantment, and the Scholarly Construction of Exorcism

In New Testament studies and related fields, an assumption whose dying has been long and slow is that ancient discourse about exorcism, the devil, and demons is rooted in a world of beliefs and practices which, seen from the distance of a more enlightened age (i.e., ours), can only be judged as 'superstitious' or 'magical'. That same assumption and others like it have had two adverse effects on previous research in the field within which the present inquiry is located. One of those effects is that scholars and students who happen to appreciate the teachings of the New Testament have sometimes been inclined to allow their distaste for what they perceive as 'magic' or 'superstition' to persuade them that such features have only a minor or non-essential place in the sacred texts. Another effect of the same distaste is that it has often militated against the serious and sustained variety of intellectual effort essential for mastering less ethnocentric and more sympathetic and illuminating ways of interpreting ancient texts and practices already packaged, pre-framed, and not infrequently devalued via their presumed association with 'magic'.[1]

Because the Gospel of John is interpreted by many scholars as including neither an account of exorcism nor ritual activities perceived to be 'magical', one could be forgiven for thinking that any discussion of 'magic' here is unnecessary. The same imagining, in fact, could be underscored by considering that the present writer identifies with a growing body of interpreters who regard much of the modern tradition of Western academic discourse about ancient 'magic' as having produced a great deal more confusion than conceptual light and clarity. So, why even permit the much-troubled term to enter the present discussion, especially from the outset? In brief, the reason the key term should be granted entry is that the interpretative scenario elaborated in the ensuing pages, when it is considered as a complex whole, is likely to be misconstrued by some readers as attributing a 'magical world-view' to the

DOI: 10.4324/9781003359319-3

Fourth Gospel, and thus to represent a theologically distasteful alternative to more familiar ways of understanding the words and actions presented in the ancient text. Partly as a preventative measure against that type of misconstrual, the analysis below can be previewed here as eschewing discourse about 'magic', and as focusing instead on the degree to which the Fourth Gospel shows interest in 'rituals of cosmic power',[2] a concept less freighted with pejorative connotations and better suited to the types of processes whose representation in the Fourth Gospel is central to the present investigation.

As just mentioned, the Fourth Gospel has often been interpreted by previous interpreters as lacking exorcism traditions,[3] and thus also as differing significantly in that respect from the Synoptics. Accordingly, but also with less conceptual caution, the same Gospel has also sometimes been described as evincing an outlook less 'magical' than that of the Synoptics,[4] each of which includes no less than three exorcism stories in the form-critical sense – the Gospel of Mark, almost certainly the earliest, has the most with four[5] – in addition to various references to exorcistic healings in the form of either narrative summaries or sayings attributed to Jesus. Specifically in regard to exorcistic references, an exception to the perspective just summarised can be seen in a few scholarly readings of the Johannine Jesus' utterance about the imminent expulsion of 'the ruler of this world' (John 12:31b), where the key clause has sometimes been construed as envisioning a triumph over Satan by means of a 'cosmic exorcism'.[6] At no point, however, between the latter reference and the end of the Fourth Gospel is either the satanic ruler or the Judas-figure he comes to inhabit (John 13:27) characterised as being expelled from the cosmos; and with weightier relevance to the interpretation developed in the pages below, neither of the interpretations just noted sees the utterance in John 12:31b as related in any meaningful way either to the departure of Judas in John 13:30 or to other actions in John 13 (e.g., Jesus' washing of the disciples' feet) that might be read as possessing special relevance for understanding the pronouncement attributed to Jesus in 12:31b.

A better approach to understanding the relationship between the Johannine expulsion of the ruler and the exorcism materials in the Synoptic Gospels can be facilitated, I suggest, by considering whether exorcism as a category might serve Gospel scholarship more fruitfully if it is defined less narrowly than usual and is allowed instead to be, like most of the conceptual categories we use every day, rather more blurry.[7] One way of making this sort of adjustment is to extend the existing narrow definition – the conception of exorcism, for instance, as an action whereby cosmic power is mediated by a human agent for the specific purpose of expelling an impure spirit understood to be the cause of illness, impurity, or other negative states of being in an individual human victim[8] – by recognising family resemblances between prototypical instances of the category in its strict sense and other phenomena which, whilst diverging from the prototype(s) in certain notable ways, resemble it in others.[9] The type of comparative analysis facilitated by such an approach has been informally hinted at above but will be pursued more systematically in the pages that follow.

Since the majority of scholars who have dealt with John 12:31b view the key clause neither as part of an exorcism story nor even as a reference to exorcism within some other literary-generic frame,[10] the present stage in my inquiry might begin most appropriately by asking why that is the case, a question tantamount to querying what it is precisely about the actions narrated in John 12–13 that diverges so far from the assumed prototype(s) of exorcism that most interpreters are unwilling to see a reference to exorcism in this part of John's Gospel. As it happens, an entire cluster of divergences can be identified that make the scholarly reticence understandable. For instance, since Judas is explicitly portrayed in John 13:27 as having become possessed by Satan, an audience familiar with the exorcistic scripts and prototypes of the Synoptic accounts would almost certainly expect any ensuing exorcistic climax in the Fourth Gospel to feature an expulsion of Satan from the body of Judas, as opposed to the actual dénouement narrated in its place (John 13:30), the focal object of motion in that context not being Satan but rather Judas, with Satan still inside him. Judas, therefore, holds the unenviable distinction of being the only demoniac figure mentioned in the Gospels that is not healed by Jesus or his followers.[11]

On the other hand, and at least to the extent that both the departure of Judas in John 13:30 and a wide range of broadly exorcistic events serve to move one type of impurity or another from one location to another, and thus belong to a category of actions termed by the late J. Z. Smith as 'rituals of relocation',[12] the aforementioned point of divergence is scarcely able to obliterate the family resemblance between the relocation of the satanically indwelt Judas and other rituals of broadly exorcistic relocation. In the Synoptic stories about the exorcism at Gerasa/Gadara, for instance, the impure spirits are transferred via exorcism into the bodies of impure animals, which in turn carry the impurity still farther away by rushing down a bank and drowning in the nearby lake.[13] In Tob. 8:1–3, the demon Asmodaios is ritually removed from the presence of Sarah of Ecbatana and relocated to Egypt. In the Yom Kippur ritual as prescribed in Leviticus 16, the iniquities of the Israelites are placed on the head of the scapegoat who in turn transfers the pollution outside the camp to the desert region haunted by Azazel,[14] a demonic power assumed to be instrumental in the people's cyclical contamination. And in John 13:30 the satanically possessed Judas and the dangerous impurities he embodies (13:10–11) are driven out from the little society of believing disciples and into the darkness of night. None of those accounts matches the exorcistic prototype perfectly, nor is any one of them identical to the others; but a family resemblance can nonetheless be recognised between them all.[15]

As a matter of methodological principle, however, points of resemblance and similarity should not be allowed to obscure potentially important areas of difference. For instance, unlike the demoniacs in the Synoptic stories, the satanically occupied betrayer in John has been known by name to the text's audience from the moment of his introduction in the larger story (John 6:64–71). Additionally, although the cultural logic of negative spirit-possession in the Synoptic accounts probably entails that the demoniacs in those contexts are incapable of exercising faith in Jesus prior to their healing,[16] the authors of the Synoptics offer at best only scant evidence of having considered that issue; whereas the Johannine Judas is portrayed both explicitly and implicitly as an unbeliever.[17] Furthermore, and yet again unlike the Synoptic demoniacs, Judas enters and exits the larger narrative of the Fourth Gospel not just once but at several different junctures, in addition to being mentioned a few times in the discourses of Jesus;[18] as a result, Judas possesses far greater prominence as a character in the Fourth Gospel than any of the various demoniacs in the Synoptics enjoys in their respective contexts.

Judas, of course, is not the only *topos* worthy of comparative analysis for purposes of the present inquiry. Indeed, potentially much greater insight might be derived by comparing the Johannine account and similar material in the Synoptics with special reference to the exorcistic agency and technique of Jesus. For instance, although the combination of utterances and actions attributed to Jesus in John 12:31b and 13:27–30 have already been interpreted above as broadly exorcistic, the agency and involvement of the Johannine Jesus in the exorcistic process is significantly less explicit than the agency of Jesus is in the Synoptic exorcism stories. Especially noteworthy in that connection is the difference concerning the usage of ἐκβάλλω, with the combination of the passive voice and agent-deletion in John 12:31 leaving unexpressed the identity of the actor/expeller, in contrast to the several occurrences of the same verb in Synoptic exorcism references where the role of actor/expeller is filled unambiguously by Jesus.[19]

The difference just observed between Johannine ambiguity and Synoptic explicitness is likewise to be observed in the domain of exorcistic technique, and more specifically regarding the use of verbal commands addressed to the impure spirit. In general, brief commands addressed to impure spirits are attested in several exorcism passages in the Synoptics, in John 13:27, and in a range of other ancient sources relating to exorcism. From a comparative angle, however, commands such as those attributed to Jesus in the Markan and Lukan accounts of the exorcism in the synagogue – Jesus rebukes the demon, saying, 'Be silent and come out of him!' (Mk 1:25; Lk. 4:35) – appear to sacrifice politeness on the altar of clarity and thus require little inferencing skill on the part of the demon-addressee; whereas the command addressed by the Johannine Jesus to the satanically possessed Judas – 'What you are about to do, do quickly!' (John 12:27) – depends almost entirely on the embedded context of utterance for its meaning and is therefore so enigmatic and unclear to everyone present except the possessed addressee that confusion and debates over its meaning immediately arise among the disciples (vv. 28–29). Nonetheless, as the agreement between the swiftness of action demanded by Jesus (τάχιον, v. 27) and the quickness of Judas' departure (εὐθύς, v. 30) confirms,[20] the broadly exorcistic aim of Jesus' command is both understood and obeyed by the addressee.[21]

Other areas of comparison could be explored in ways that might sharpen our perception of the family-resemblance between exorcisms in the narrow sense and the expulsion of Judas in John 13:30; but the particular blendings of similarity and difference treated above should suffice to indicate the broadly exorcistic character of the happenings presented in John 12:31b and 13:1–32 (esp. vv. 21–30).

Notwithstanding the intrinsic interest of recognising the exorcistic features in this part of John's Gospel, however, there are strong reasons for thinking the earliest audiences of John 12–13 would have been prompted by various features in the text to hear it not merely as the narration of a broadly exorcistic relocation of Judas/RW but also as an event possessing paradigmatic and ritual implications for Christ communities in the setting of the Fourth Gospel's earliest audience. Those sorts of implications are best approached by first noting a linguistic feature highlighted in John 13 but not yet discussed in the present analysis: namely, the role of eucharistic bread and the little 'morsel' (ψωμίον, John 13:26–30) in Jesus' interactions with Judas/RW and the other characters in this setting.

How to Do Things with Bread

The Greek noun often rendered as 'sop' or 'piece of bread', ψωμίον, occurs four times in John 13:26–30,[22] solely in reference to the bit of food Jesus gives to Judas near the end of the supper, but is not attested elsewhere in the New Testament. In the larger narrative of the meal in John 13:1–30, the term belongs to a set of lexemes – ἄρτος, δεῖπνον, ἀνάκειμαι, τρώγω, ἑορτή, and πάσχα – collocated in a manner appropriate to the given meal scene;[23] and more generally, both the diminutive used in the present passage and the non-diminutive cognate (ψωμός) are used in ancient Greek to denote either scraps of food, the substance of which (when it is indicated) varies according to context but often is bread.[24] Yet the combination of the term's repetition in so brief a stretch of the Johannine narrative, the limitation of its usage in 13:26–30 to the item given solely to Judas in particular, and its semantic potential in a context where ἄρτος would have been a suitable but also less marked selection,[25] all work together to give the word a level of salience it normally lacks in other ancient settings of its usage. But what significance in this context might it have, if any, beyond its markedness?

Published exegesis on John 13:26–30 has been reticent to make much of the morsel, but a couple of interpretative possibilities are worth mentioning as conjectures for future discussion and evaluation. First, although the diminutive form used in John (ψωμίον) is unattested in the LXX, the base form of the same noun, ψωμός, occurs in twelve passages supported in each case by two or more of the main witnesses to the LXX;[26] and one of those passages – namely, the story in 1 Samuel 28 about King Saul's consultation of the female medium at Endor – not only was generally well-known[27] but includes a combination of motifs likewise found in key portions of John 12–13. From a comparative perspective, the following blend of features in LXX 1 Samuel 28 is especially interesting. Like Judas in John 13, Saul is offered something to eat (ψωμὸν ἄρτου, v. 22) by a well-intentioned mediator-figure directly after receiving prophetic truth about the tragedy he is about to experience (vv. 16–19). After taking some food, and again similar to Judas, Saul departs from the setting of his meal in the darkness of night (v. 25). Just as Judas' presence at the meal in John 13 is implicitly deceitful (v. 18), Saul's nocturnal visit with the medium at Endor is marked by secrecy and deception (vv. 9–10). In the antecedent co-texts of these stories, moreover, the key characters – Judas and Saul – have already been portrayed as behaving under the influence of noxious spirit beings;[28] Saul, in fact, comes closer than any other character in the Hebrew Bible to being a demoniac like those met in the Synoptic Gospels, and Judas is the only character described by the narrator of the Fourth Gospel as possessed by Satan. Significantly, though, and unlike the demoniacs who encounter Jesus in the Synoptic narratives, both Judas and Saul alike are characterised as never experiencing a conclusive release from the agents of their spirit-afflictions. Furthermore, and at least partly as a result of their uniquely close association with evil spirits, both Judas and Saul pursue murderous plots against anointed figures (i.e., Jesus and David) understood by some to be legitimate successors to the royal throne of Israel.[29] And if Judas' departure in John 13:30 is understood (as defended here) as a fulfilment of the prediction in John 12:31 about the expulsion of 'the ruler of this world', then both Saul and Judas are to be seen as emblems of an old political order about to be succeeded by a better type of rule.[30] But perhaps most significantly for the present study, since the intertextual linkage just outlined would give special prominence to the correspondence between Judas and King Saul as demoniacally tainted characters, it would also offer at least indirect support to the thesis that the portrayal of Judas' withdrawal from the meal scene in John 13:30 is best understood as the denouement of a broadly exorcistic event.

One other possible function of the repetition of ψωμίον in John 13:26–30 deserves mention. Although the temporal setting given in John 13:1 for the ensuing meal militates against the event being identified as a Passover meal, other features indicate that the event has nonetheless been conceptualised along the ceremonial lines of the Christ-group's eucharistic meetings, one of whose main functions was to strengthen group solidarity and oneness;[31] but as hinted above, since the dining event in John 13 is also portrayed as part of a ritual process for dealing with Judas as a singular source of discord and impurity, the use of a different noun to designate the food that he alone is given by Jesus at the end of the meal has potential to reinforce the image of Judas as lacking true solidarity with the group. Of the several participants in the Johannine meal event, Judas alone is described as having been given 'a morsel', a distinction probably arising in part from his being the only figure at the meal who does not properly share in the Christ-group's commensality.[32]

However, viewed from within the wider context of ancient near eastern and Mediterranean exorcistic practices, the morsel in John 13:26–30 is hardly extraordinary; for it is paralleled by the use of food items and other materials in a wide range of exorcistic and related events in antiquity. In the Synoptic accounts about the exorcism in Gerasa/Gadara, for instance, the spirits are transferred from the demoniac(s) into the bodies of nearby swine which promptly transport the spirits into the nearby lake/sea;[33] and in Tob. 8:1–3 the heart and liver of a large fish are used successfully by Tobias, son of Tobit and Anna, to liberate Sarah of Ecbatana from the murderous attentions of the demon Asmodeus. In other exorcistic contexts, edibles ranging from pure wine, olive oil, saffron, coriander, and water, to foodstuffs appropriate for an Egyptian-Hittite festival are mentioned.[34] Also attested are non-food items: roots, ashes from a red cow, finger-rings, amulets, water-pots, leather flasks, statues, stones, articles of clothing previously touched by a renowned human agent of cosmic power, and uncanny epistles addressed with foreknowledge to the demon in advance of the exorcistic occasion.[35] The magico-ritual worldview assumed in the exorcistic use of these objects should not be denigrated as somehow inferior to or far-removed from the perspective of the Fourth Gospel; for the little morsel in John 13 not only plays an essential role in one of the Gospel's depictions of Jesus as a reliable prophet – Jesus knows in advance that his betrayer will be the one to whom he is about to give the morsel (13:26) – but also is linked by the Gospel's narrator so closely to the circumstances of Judas' withdrawal that it is difficult not to view the morsel as instrumental in that action (13:30).[36]

However, since the Johannine Judas' departure from the group (13:30) serves well by itself to set the stage for his subsequent role in the arrest of Jesus (18:3, 5), critical readers may rightly wonder what purpose (if any) is served by the details about Jesus' giving of the morsel, Satan's entry into Judas, Jesus' enigmatic command, and Judas' taking of the morsel. What value would be lost if the narrative were reduced to Jesus commanding Judas more directly, as indeed he does back in John 12:7, and Judas immediately withdrawing into the night? From the perspective of the present argument, one response to that question is that the imagined simplification would probably diminish the exorcistic nature of a sequence of events (i.e., John 13:26–30) that needs to fulfil the Johannine Jesus' prior prediction of something akin to an exorcism (John 12:31). But more importantly for the analysis below, John 13 contains several strong hints that the exorcistic removal of Judas/RW from the Jesus circle is only one of several interrelated aims pursued by Jesus in vv. 26–30 and the immediate co-text; and critical awareness of one of those aims in particular has potential to illuminate the relevance and function of several of the details – most especially but not exclusively, those concerning the morsel – in those same verses.

Experiential Distance and Ritual Paradigm

The Johannine Jesus' interest in protecting the purity of the believing disciples as a group has attracted much scholarly comment and was noted briefly above. That particular interest is unlikely to have been peculiar to the Johannine Jesus' context of reference; indeed, the way in which the purity theme is presented in John 13 is almost certainly the product of a critical rethinking of purity concepts in the interest of managing the situation addressed by the author of the Gospel. To understand how the emergent concepts of purity and cleansing in John 13 might illuminate the significance of the morsel and other details in vv. 26–30 in particular, a motivation not yet mentioned needs to be recognised in the author's composition of this material: namely, that of demonstrating a paradigm of in-group ritual action which, after Jesus returns to the Father and is no longer directly accessible, can be performed to cleanse the group and protect it against the devil and his impure schemes. Evidence for the existence of this aim is discernible in the form of what some linguists call 'experiential distance', the particular facet of register involving the conceptual proximity of the language choices made in a given situation to the non-verbal processes taking place in the same setting.[37] Specifically in John 13, the Passover meal is taking place and Jesus has begun to wash the disciples feet; but the Johannine Jesus, in addition to making experientially low-distance references to the meal and the washing, sprinkles his discourse with conspicuously higher-distance references to the disciples' future understanding of present events (v. 7), to an act of betrayal that is yet to take place (vv. 11, 21–28), to Jesus' present ritual action being followed as an example in the future (v. 15), to Jesus' followers being blessed in the future as a result of following his example (v. 17), to the future experience of continuing to believe in Jesus after Judas' still future act of betrayal (v. 19), to individuals in the future receiving emissaries sent by Jesus (v. 20), and to future circumstances in which Jesus will no longer be with his disciples as he was before his crucifixion but will nonetheless be recognised and honoured as a result of the reciprocal love displayed by them (vv. 32–35). Furthermore, while much of the distance in those features is temporal in nature, one of its effects is to help the audience imagine a range of spatially distanced situations, potentially outside of Judea, in which this part of the Gospel narrative (i.e., John 13) could be relevant.

Cumulatively, all of that adds up to a considerable measure of experiential distance, both temporally and circumstantially, in John 13:1–35.[38] With the motif of the morsel thus being closely tied to the still-future act of betrayal, and since the absence of the morsel from the Synoptics increases the likelihood of its presence in John 13:26–30 being a motivated invention, the Johannine Jesus' use of the morsel points beyond its own immediate context of reference and contributes to the formation of a model of how Jesus-groups in the implied situation of the Fourth Gospel should deal with any figures like Judas they might find in their assemblies. In brief, one of the main aims of the assembly's practice of the eucharist should be to maintain proper order in the group by dealing with – or even excluding – any uncooperative, free-riding, or potentially polluting types at the meeting.[39]

A noteworthy strength of the reading just suggested is that it has potential for supporting a fresh blend of old and new ideas regarding how the Johannine Jesus' washing of the disciples' feet might be best understood. At least nine different readings of the footwashing are summarised in the influential commentary by Brown;[40] but as already hinted above, the broadly exorcistic understanding of John 12:31 and 13:30 defended in the present study affords more support to the eucharistic interpretation[41] than to the familiar alternatives. More specifically, since Judas is clearly implied by Jesus in John 13:10–11 to be pervasively unclean, and with the group-purifying relocation of Judas in 13:26–30 having been facilitated in part by processes involving the morsel (13:26–30), linked as it is to the bread in 13:18 and 6:1–59, eucharistic overtones are likely to have formed at least part of the significance inferred by early audiences of the footwashing episode in 13:1–30.[42]

Parts, however, must not be confused with wholes, either in our thinking and talking about the human body in general or in the present effort to interpret the footwashing symbolism in John 13; and for reasons worth exploring at least briefly here, the eucharistic associations discussed above should probably be understood as only one level of a multi-layered and more richly symbolic episode whose potential significance can be illuminated both by other portions of the present analysis and by its chosen methodology. As for other sections of the present study, the prophecy-fulfilment scheme proposed in the preceding chapters entails that one of the most salient processes described in John 12:31–13:30 is the exorcistic relocating of Judas – a disciple characterised not just once but twice in 13:10–11 as unclean – from a place inside the social body of the Jesus group to the worldly space outside it; and in the chapter of analysis following this one, that same exorcistic process is interpreted as serving simultaneously as an instance of community discipline (by exclusion of an unruly member from a sacred meal) comparable to that practised by many ancient Mediterranean associations. Those two observations, taken together, give rise to a potentially fruitful question which to my knowledge has never been asked in scholarly exegesis of the footwashing episode: namely, how likely can it be that Jesus' removal of dirt from the disciples' feet in John 13:5–11 has no definably meaningful relation to the removal of Judas – the one wholly unclean disciple (13:10–11) – from the Jesus circle as conceptualised in John 12:31–13:30, in the larger frame, that is, within which the footwashing is embedded, and from which it surely derives a good measure of its significance?

The value of that question resides not merely in its capacity to answer itself – Jesus' embodied performance of washing dirt off the disciples' feet has outstanding potential to work as a metaphor for his less straightforward, more complicated action of purifying the social body of his disciples by excluding the unclean member – but even more so in the hints it provides concerning how the relevant aspects of the footwashing work together as a performative blend of body-related metaphors. As just suggested, for instance, the dirt that is implicitly but clearly present, conceptually, in the footwashing can now be seen as a metaphor for Judas; and from the perspective of the Gospel's narrator, that is a very apt metaphor indeed. From that same conceptualisation, moreover, it directly follows that Jesus' washing of the disciples' feet is a performative metaphor for his imminent exorcistic cleansing of the group from the polluting presence of Judas. And finally, once the footwashing story is understood as a metaphorical source domain for meanings pertaining to the exorcistic cleansing and group-discipline performed by the Johannine Jesus, the part-whole structure of the feet-body discourse in the footwashing can easily be interpreted as a metaphor for conceptualising

Jesus' disciples as individual members of the larger social body – the Jesus circle as a collective entity in the text – from which Judas comes to be excluded.

Among the various kinds of support that could be offered in a full articulation of the present interpretation, considerations of textual proximity – the footwashing story is, literally, not merely close to the prophecy-fulfilment scheme but is embedded in it – and the prominence of body discourse, explicit at some points and implicit at others, in both the source and target domains (i.e., footwashing and exorcistic exclusion) are especially weighty and deserve more attention than I can give to them here. But in addition to those sources of support, at least one other facet of the Johannine footwashing discourse demands attention that has potential to give additional strength to the present reading.

The facet in question is the Johannine Jesus' clear insistence that his own action of washing the disciples' feet, whatever reading of it one might adopt, should serve as a 'paradigm' (ὑπόδειγμα, 13:15) for the interpersonal behaviour of the Jesus circle's members (13:12–17). As Jesus has washed his disciples' feet, so likewise the disciples 'ought to wash one another's feet' (13:14). The prescriptive nature and force of the footwashing, as a paradigm, is matched in greater and lesser degrees by the various interpretations proposed in modern critical studies of that episode. For instance, and strictly as a model for in-group behaviour, the footwashing almost certainly coheres less with the baptismal interpretation – should in-group members be baptising others who likewise are already in-group members? – than with a thoroughly eucharistic reading.[43] But at this stage in the present inquiry, the question is: how well does my 'exorcistic discipline and relocation' reading cohere, if at all, with the prescriptive model/paradigm requirement? In anticipation of the fuller treatment of association meals and discipline in the next chapter, it may suffice here to observe that, if the footwashing episode is construed as a metaphoric paradigm that enjoins an in-group audience of Christ-followers to practise collective responsibility at their meetings for expelling any members who exemplify unfaithful attitudes or behaviour, that same construal has excellent potential to serve as a code of discipline for the group and thus coheres with the paradigm criterion at least as well as any of the more familiar proposals do.

As the metaphorical dirt to be removed from the other disciples' feet, the Johannine Judas derives no benefit either from Jesus' performance of footwashing or from the eucharistic morsel he subsequently receives from Jesus in the same setting. Judas is, moreover, the only disciple at the meal whose condition in that context is described as requiring not a mere washing of the feet but instead a holistic bathing (13:10–11); for as implied by Jesus in 13:10, anyone still unbathed would need the full sort of washing requested – but not needed – by Peter in 13:9. Since what the

Johannine Judas therefore needs is a thorough bathing (13:10) – probably best understood as a metaphorical effect of exercising faith in Jesus'[44] – he is most unlikely to be rescued or otherwise aided by the eucharist, which is implied by the sequencing of 13:27 ('After the morsel Satan entered into him') to have been a determining factor in his becoming possessed by Satan. The Johannine Judas' evident immunity to any benefit deriving from either the footwashing or the eucharistic morsel, therefore, holds those two concepts tightly together and thus reinforces the proposal above that the morsel is part of the target domain whose sources of meaning are supplied in good measure by the footwashing story.[45]

Consequences and Co-Text

Neither the co-text of the Fourth Gospel's footwashing-exorcism blend nor even the implications of the reading suggested for it above can be treated comprehensively within the scope of a study such as this one. The interpretation outlined above, however, has potential to impact understanding of John 13:31–21:25 in at least a few ways that should not escape present notice.

In addition to affording him no protection against eventual destruction,[46] the Johannine Judas' reception of the eucharistic morsel initiates a development in his characterisation whereby certain implications of his diabolical identity become more apparent. His departure into the night (13:30), as discussed above, is simultaneously a move out from the Jesus circle and signals his status as an outsider, an unbeliever, a non-member of the in-group. The ensuing shift by Jesus to the theme of reciprocal love (13:34–38), verbally conceptualised for the first time in the Gospel immediately after Judas' withdrawal, is timed in a manner that suggests it would have had little or no relevance to Judas, whose unbelief (6:64) is probably understood to entail inability on his part to fathom the type of love enjoined by Jesus to the other disciples in that context;[47] indeed, as Jesus warns later in the same discourse, 'the world' over which the diabolical ruler, now dwelling within Judas, exercises his power is one that not only lacks love for the Jesus group but actively hates it (15:19). However, with an apparent climax of Judas' ritual exclusion being reached in 13:30 ('he immediately went out'), the process of his relocation is conceptualised shortly afterwards in terms that entail he is no longer inside the container – the social body, that is, constituted by Jesus' followers – but instead is now outside of it; more precisely, in John 14:30 he is said by Jesus to be 'coming' (i.e., to Jesus and his circle) and thus is not seen in the immediate context of Jesus' utterance as still residing within the social circle of the disciples.[48] And finally, when that same process of return reaches its climax in John 18:3, Judas/RW is portrayed as having guided an armed subdivision of Roman soldiers, accompanied by Judean police, to Jesus and the disciples, with great symbolic weight being loaded by the narrator onto Judas' positioning of himself close in space to the posse set against Jesus (18:5).[49]

Indirectly, therefore, the foregoing summary of key developments in the Johannine characterisation of Judas after he is given the morsel in John 13:26–30 strengthens a proposal made at the beginning of the present study: namely, the predicted expulsion of 'the ruler of this world' is realised in his removal not to some place outside the *cosmos*, but rather from inside the Jesus circle out into 'the world', into a space associated at other points in the Fourth Gospel with darkness,[50] and thus outside the social body of Jesus' true followers. Therein is to be seen, moreover, a type of motif present in many stories involving exorcistic events. In the Synoptic story about the man liberated from Legion, for instance, the relocation of the impure spirits includes their transfer into the swine who proceed to rush into the lake and drown (Mk 5:1–20 and par.); in Tobit, the relocation of the demon Asmodeus culminates in his being bound in Egypt (8:1–3); and in the Fourth Gospel, the relocating of Judas – embodiment of the diabolical ruler – sees him aligned in the end, both spatially and ideologically, with the worldly system of imperial power operative in Judea (18:3–5) that hates and persecutes both Jesus and his authentic followers (15:18–25).[51]

From the perspective of the implied authors of all of those stories, none of the destinations for the relocated spirits is a place of blessing; and the unrelenting disapproval associated with Judas in particular throughout his appearances in John 6 – 17 eventually serves as, *inter alia*, a reservoir of rhetorical power for shaming the custodians of Roman order in John 18:3–4, where the latter are portrayed as having been guided by Judas – a satanically possessed embodiment of 'the ruler of this world' ever since he left the Jesus circle (13:30)[52] – to the setting of Jesus' eventual seizure. The discrediting of all the forces aligned against Jesus in the Johannine narration of the arrest becomes weightier in the immediately ensuing clauses where Jesus' use of ἐγώ εἰμι without a predicate ('I am', 18:5), as an appropriation of God's own self-designation,[53] is implied to have caused the entire search party to draw backwards and fall before Jesus to the ground (ἔπεσαν χαμαί, 18:6).[54] By comparison then with both the prediction of the expulsion (12:31) and its fulfilment (13:30), whose presentation has been interpreted above as relying far more heavily on container metaphors than on orientational schemas, the collective fall narrated in John 18:6 constitutes a striking deviation in conceptual mode, with the downward movement entailed by the use of πίπτω suggesting a failure or defeat as in numerous other ancient contexts in which that verb is employed.[55] The shift from the in/out schema used earlier[56] to the up/down orientation in 18:6 is probably best explained, at least partly, as being motivated by considerations of metaphorical coherence; for in contrast to the Johannine Judas prior to his withdrawal in 13:30, none of the parties portrayed as falling in 18:6 – the ruler, the Roman maniple, the Jerusalem police, and (in this new setting of the garden) now also Judas – are understood to have been Christ-group insiders directly before their collapse.

But just as importantly, among the several occurrences of the verb πίπτω with similar connotations in the LXX,[57] one shares enough lexical and conceptual space with the Johannine arrest scene and its immediate co-text that the possibility of an echo or allusion is worth considering. LXX Psalm 90 (91 in the MT), whose Hebrew forms are known to have been adapted for apotropaic use against demons at Qumran and in other ancient Jewish contexts,[58] not only includes a promise of protection for those who know the divine name (LXX Psalm 90:14) but also identifies the relevant adversaries as including both demonic entities (90:5–6) and human foes who 'will fall' (90:7) in their thousands at the feet of the protected faithful.[59] The strong emphasis on divine protection both in the Psalm itself and in its ancient reception give it a high level of appropriateness for adaptation in a context where the Jesus circle's need for protection against the schemes of the evil one is mentioned repeatedly, both in the prayer of Jesus (John 17:11–15) and in its narrative co-text (John 18:7–9).

The narrated events just mentioned are presented in John 13:31–21:25 as foreknown by Jesus and as fulfilling the plan(s) of God as disclosed in Jewish Scripture. But a necessary condition for that same flow of events can be identified in the exclusion of Judas, narrated in John 13:30 as the realisation of Jesus' prior prediction about the satanic ruler (12:31); for unless Judas leaves the Jesus circle, how will he be able to fulfil the prophecy of betrayal? Through what process will the authorities in Jerusalem come to perceive Jesus as a threat to the prevailing order? By what mechanism will Jesus come to be crucified, as 'the lamb of God who takes away the sin of the world'? And what then about the resurrection? In brief, if Judas is not driven out, how will Jesus' be lifted up? A historical imagination informed by the Synoptic Gospels and other ancient sources could of course conceive alternative paths towards the same theological end; but in terms of the Fourth Gospel as we have it, the questions just asked not only heighten the prominence of Judas' exorcistic relocation in the rhetoric and plot of the Gospel but also have potential to foreground the particular means by which that same process of expulsion is achieved. As one of a couple of those means, but also in anticipation of the next chapter of analysis, the eucharistic morsel deserves additional comment here; and as part of a reference chain that links the footwashing and expulsion narratives in John 13 to Jesus' discourse about the vineyard and the vine-grower in John 15, the concept of Jesus' word or speech likewise merits attention as a means of efficacious action in the same episode.

As several commentators have pointed out who infer eucharistic overtones from the morsel in John 13:26–30, decades prior to the composition of the Fourth Gospel the eucharist is understood by Paul in 1 Cor. 11:27–34 as having power not only to benefit participants of suitable attitude but also to induce illness in any who partake of the meal 'without discerning the body' (1 Cor. 11:29).[60] According to that understanding, and offended as Judas and the other unbelieving disciples in John 6 are by the thought of Jesus' flesh and blood as food and drink (6:52–65), Judas himself and anyone like him would more likely experience harm by partaking of the eucharist than healing. In that connection, it is worth adding that although the Fourth Gospel has no parallel to the Matthean tradition about Judas' suicidal end (Mt. 27:3–10), it does have Jesus highlighting Judas' individual infamy as the only one of those whom Jesus was given that in the end was lost (John 17:12), an outcome perhaps even worse than suicide from the perspective of the Fourth Gospel's implied author. As explored in the next chapter of analysis, both the inglorious end of the Johannine Judas and the role of the morsel in bringing it about are two of several motifs whose significance in the Fourth Gospel can be illuminated further by reading John 12:31; 13:1–30; and select portions of their narrative co-text in the light of recent historical scholarship on Graeco-Roman clubs and associations, the form and order of their banqueting events, and evidence of their interest in good order and rules for disciplining uncooperative members.

In the brief sequence of events directly preceding the departure of the Johannine Judas (13:26–30), the activity of Jesus that leads to the expulsion includes not only the giving of the morsel but also the word of command he speaks to Judas – 'what you are about to do, do quickly' (v. 27) – an utterance which, as it is addressed to a character now satanically possessed, has far greater potential to be understood as an exorcistic spell than most commentators allow.[61] That same utterance, moreover, is normally understood to possess no special salience within the larger narrative framework either of the Fourth Gospel as a whole or even of John 13:1–30 in particular; but since a structurally salient part of that same framework has been redefined above as a prophecy-fulfilment scheme whose climax consists at least partly of an exorcistic cleansing of the Jesus circle, the word of command uttered by Jesus directly before Judas' climactic response should probably be construed as carrying much heavier semantic freight than commentators on this episode tend to imagine. As outlined below, the same reassessment is supported by considering the potential contribution of the utterance in 13:27 to reference chains and lexical strings which tie various parts of the footwashing-exclusion narrative (13:1–30) to Jesus' teaching in John 15:1–8 about the vineyard and the vine-grower.[62]

After introducing the metaphors of the vineyard, the vine-grower, and the vines (15:1–2), the Johannine Jesus proceeds to develop his topic of discourse in 15:3 by:

i making his intratextual audience of disciples the focus and grammatical subject of his next clause (ὑμεῖς ... ὑμῖν, 15:3);
ii using two words from a single lexical group – καθαίρει ('prunes' or 'cleanses', 15:2) and καθαροί ('clean', 15:3) – whose repetition in 15:2–3 contributes to a striking instance of paronomasia and gives a heightened sense of importance to the concepts instantiated by those words in their given context; and
iii embedding the second, adjectival form of those same two words in a brief syntactical structure – ὑμεῖς καθαροί ἐστε ('you [plural reference to the disciples] are clean') – whose only other occurrence in the Gospel is found in John 13:10, where the contrast between Judas and the other disciples regarding purity is highlighted in the setting of the footwashing.

Owing largely to the second and third features just noted, a cohesive tie between Jesus' utterances in John 13:10 and 15:3 tends to be acknowledged at least briefly by scholarly commentators;[63] but the degree to which that same tie might make Judas relevant to the interpretation of John 15:3 and its immediate co-text is a question on which critical opinion varies significantly.[64] By focusing on that question here, the present inquiry intends to show that the exorcistic purification thesis enhances the interpretation of subsequent portions of the Gospel such as John 15:1–8 by illuminating frequently overlooked connexions between that passage, the narration of Judas' purificatory exclusion, and the 'word' of Jesus by which that exclusion is achieved.

In John 15:3 the purity attributed by Jesus to his post-exorcism addressees is described as having been achieved 'by the word' (διὰ τὸν λόγον) he had spoken to them. Although part of Jesus' utterance in that context is widely understood as effecting a cohesive tie to the identical construction in John 13:10 (i.e., ὑμεῖς καθαροί ἐστε), the phrase διὰ τὸν λόγον is interpreted by most scholars not as requiring any particular instance of Jesus' prior utterances to be the intended referent but rather as a more general reference to all of the communicative action attributed to Jesus up to that point in the Fourth Gospel.[65] However, because the grammatical correspondence between 13:10 and 15:3 has potential to recall most especially the contrast between Judas and the other disciples in 13:10–11,[66] but also in light of the evidence summarised above for the exclusion in 13:30 having elevated importance in the rhetoric of John 12–13, the word of command addressed by Jesus to Judas in 13:27 should probably be recognised as occupying a central place in the larger 'word' mentioned in 15:3.[67]

Against that interpretation, the absence of overt reference to Judas in John 15:1–8 might seem to weigh heavily. That sort of critique, however, would miss the central feature of the present proposal, which is not that Judas is either explicitly or implicitly present in John 15 but rather that the 'given' or 'old' purity discourse of 13:10–30 is picked up and blended in 15:1–8 with the textually 'new' viticultural metaphors to expand on the problem illustrated earlier, in John 13, regarding Judas. The nature of the progression from the former unit to the latter, therefore, is a movement from the particular example (i.e., Judas) to the general phenomenon (i.e., fruitless 'vines' in the 'vineyard'). And therein lies yet another source of support for the present exorcism-purification-exclusion interpretation of John 12:31 and 13:1–30; for the prophecy-fulfilment scheme on which that interpretation rests entails that not only the satanic ruler but also Judas, as the ruler's metaphorical container (13:27), is to be 'driven out' (ἐκβληθήσεται ἔξω, 12:31), with the exorcistic lexis of Jesus' prediction in John 12:31 being echoed in the subsequent description of what happens to 'vines' that do not bear fruit (15:3, 6). More precisely, such vines are taken away by the vine-grower and 'thrown out' (ἐβλήθη ἔξω, 15:6) of the vineyard, with the process of their removal being highlighted in that context (15:6) by a repetition of βάλλω where the second occurrence of the verb (εἰς τὸ πῦρ βάλλουσιν) contributes less to the information value of its clause than to the strength of the lexical tie between 15:6 and 12:31.

Thus, while Judas is not to be seen, physically, at any point in Jesus' teaching about the vineyard and the vines, the effects of his characterisation in the Fourth Gospel up to John 13:30 (or perhaps even 14:31) – and most especially the climactic narration of his withdrawal/exclusion from the Jesus circle – can nonetheless be discerned in Jesus' teaching in John 15:1–8 about unproductive vines. Indeed, according to the reading offered here, the Johannine Judas should probably be seen as, amongst other things, a prototype of the unproductive vine. But just as importantly, since every unproductive vine in the Jesus vineyard is described in 15:1–2 as being removed specifically by Jesus' Father – the metaphorical vine-grower – those same metaphors have potential for clarifying a question of agency raised by the syntax of Jesus' prediction in 12:31, a question which to my knowledge is yet to be given satisfactory treatment in published exegesis.

The question of agency in John 12:31 is likely to produce the best exegetical fruit if it is framed in terms of why a specifically passive-voice form of the verb ἐκβάλλω, signifying the process of the ruler's future expulsion, was selected for use in that context with no attendant indication regarding the nature or identity of the agent. That question can be approached to good effect by exploring how agency is conceptualised at three different points in the literary co-text of Jesus' prediction in John 12:31: namely, in John 13:5–15 (i.e., the footwashing), in 13:30 (i.e., Judas' withdrawal), and in 15:1–6 (i.e., the vineyard and the vine-grower), each of which has been construed above as including its own retrospective conceptualisation of the exorcistic process envisioned by Jesus back in John 12:31. For purposes of optimal explanation, the third of those passages is discussed first.

In John 15:1–6, it is clear that the character/participant who uproots every unproductive vine in the vineyard is the Father of the Johannine Jesus, as the metaphorical vine grower, a representation whose clarity helps to disambiguate the less explicit identity of the agent in the action of unproductive group-members being 'thrown out like a vine' (ἐβλήθη ἔξω ὡς τὸ κλῆμα) in v. 6. In the latter clause too, therefore, the actor of determinative force is best identified as the Father. In John 13:5–15, however, whose account of the footwashing has been interpreted above as a source domain of purity metaphors for framing the expulsion of Judas in that same setting as a process of cleansing the Jesus circle, the only agent of determinative action in the clauses describing the footwashing is Jesus. And in John 13:30 yet another, third way of conceptualising agency in the clauses depicting Judas' relocation is offered, with an agency of self-determined action being attributed to Judas in the clause ἐξῆλθεν εὐθύς ('he immediately went out'), a behavioural process very similar to that ascribed to demonic spirits in several references to exorcism in the Synoptic Gospels and the Acts of the Apostles.[68]

In the three descriptions just summarised, what can defensibly be abstracted as a single event – a process broadly exorcistic in nature – is represented in three different but potentially complementary ways whose variations arise partly from features in the participant structure of the relevant clauses. Those same kinds of features nearly suffice on their own, without help from the various other types of linguistic resources deployed across the same clauses, to present the relocation of Judas as involving a multiplicity of determining agents: namely, as indicated in the foregoing analysis, Jesus, the Father, and Judas himself. By handling in that manner the question of agency in the relocation of Judas, the author of the Fourth Gospel avoids any simplistic, monocausal view about what happens in the world of his narrative, how those happenings come about, and why.

But just as importantly, by means of that same complex of synergetic agencies, the author of the Fourth Gospel clears a path for his audience to move towards a satisfying interpretation of the instance of agent-deletion, ambiguity, and mystery in the transitivity of Jesus' prediction back in John 12:31. In the first place, the silence of the Johannine Jesus regarding the assumed agent(s) responsible for the predicted expulsion makes good communicative sense in terms of the so-called 'maxim of quantity' – one of the four main constitutive dicta in H. P. Grice's 'cooperative principle' – a maxim that describes effective communicative behaviour as providing neither more information than is necessary, nor less, for achieving the communicative aims relevant in a given context of utterance.[69] In that light, and specifically in the stead of the concise clause present in John 12:31, any alternative construction specifying one or more of the various agencies and instruments mentioned in the subsequent references to the relocation would have resulted in a lengthier clause, one that almost certainly would either have flouted the maxim of quantity (e.g., by lengthening the clause to provide an explicit preview of all of the relevant agents) or have previewed the agents in an arbitrarily selective way that poorly anticipates their diversity in the subsequent references to the relocation of Judas/RW.[70] In contrast, by leaving entirely open the question of agency in 12:31, and thus also allowing the representational function of the key clause to be hazy, the Johannine Jesus increases the potential of his own prophetic utterance to find its satisfaction in a state of affairs conceptualised in diverse ways at multiple points later in the Fourth Gospel.

Additionally, interpreters of these same passages should probably see neither a compositional accident nor an instance of functional irrelevancy in the positioning of the Fourth Gospel's most ambiguous reference to the relocation of Judas and the satanic ruler (i.e., John 12:31). That same reference not only is positioned in the Gospel's first of several descriptions of the relocation event but also, appropriate to its position at the start of the sequence, is the only reference framed in the style of a prediction. As a result, the instance of agent-deletion and the consequent ambiguity in the prediction has potential to pique the audience's curiosity as to how the expectation will be fulfilled, and specifically who or what will bring it to pass. Those same qualities of ambiguity and imprecision, moreover, exemplify a long-recognised and more widely observed tendency of oracular performance that sometimes drew criticism from educated observers in the Fourth Gospel's wider context of ancient Mediterranean culture;[71] but that, of course, is a topic addressed by others in much greater detail than is warranted here.

Notes

1 The difficulty is only one facet of what Charles Taylor has detailed in his account of the present secular age of disenchantment, whose 'buffered self ... no longer fears demons, spirits, magic forces', and for whom 'these no longer impinge' or even exist. See Charles Taylor, *A Secular Age* (Cambridge, MA: The Belknap Press, 2007), 134–35 and passim.

2 On the advantages of 'ritual', or 'rituals of cosmic power', over 'magic' as a category of analysis, see J. Z. Smith, 'Trading Places', in *Ancient Magic and Ritual Power*, ed. M. W. Meyer and P. A. Mirecki (Leiden: E. J. Brill, 1995), 21–27; and several other essays in the same collection.

3 E.g., Brown, *John I–XII*, 477, reimagines the exorcistic victory of John 12:31 as 'the gradual work of believing Christians' in their fight against evil, a suggestion far more general than that developed herein; and regarding John

13:30, neither Wengst, *Das Johannes-evangelium*, II, 114–15; Bultmann, *The Gospel of John*, 482–83; nor Carson, *The Gospel according to John*, 475–76, sees wider interpretative implications in the satanically possessed condition of the Judas'-figure at the moment of his withdrawal from the Jesus circle.

4 See, e.g., Plumer, 'The Absence of Exorcisms', 356–61.
5 Mk 1:21–28; 5:1–20; 7:24–30; and 9:14–29.
6 See, e.g., A. van Oudtshoorn, 'Where Have All the Demons Gone? The Role and Place of the Devil in the Gospel of John', *Neotestamentica* 51 (2017): 77–80.
7 On the potential advantages of thinking with categories that are flexible and open rather than rigid and hard-edged, see Lakoff and Johnson, *Metaphors We Live By*, 122–25; and M. Carrithers, *Why Humans Have Cultures: Explaining Anthropology and Social Diversity* (Oxford: Oxford University Press, 1992), 12–33.
8 I.e., a precise but also comparatively constricted definition like that used for different purposes in Klutz, *The Exorcism Stories in Luke-Acts*, 4 and passim.
9 As explained by Lakoff and Johnson, *Metaphors We Live By*, 122–25; and *Philosophy in the Flesh*, 177–78, the cognitive activity of adjusting the boundaries of an existing category for a given purpose is something human beings do routinely and often unconsciously; but for many kinds of analytical activities, critical awareness of what we are doing with our categories can help us to use them more productively.
10 E.g., Schnelle, *Das Evangelium nach Johannes*, 228, sees the reference to the expulsion of the ruler (12:31) as a way of talking about a universal change of rule and the enthronement of Jesus; while Lincoln's discussion (*The Gospel according to St John*, 352) focuses almost exclusively on the cosmic trial, judgement, and reversal motifs in the preceding clause and immediate co-text.
11 Although the demoniac son in Mk 9:14–29 and parallels (Mt. 17:14–18 and Lk. 9:37–43a) proves to be a difficult case for the disciples, he is portrayed in all three versions of that story as eventually being healed exorcistically by Jesus; and outside the Gospels is the narrative of exorcistic failure attributed in Acts 19:13–20 to Paul's Jewish itinerant competitors in Ephesus.
12 J. Z. Smith, 'Towards Interpreting the Demonic Powers in Hellenistic and Roman Antiquity', *ANRW* II.16.1, 428–29.
13 Mt. 8:28–34; Mk 5:1–20; and Lk 8:26–39.
14 Cf. B. A. Levine, *In the Presence of the Lord: A Study of Cult and Some Cultic Terms in Ancient Israel* (SJLA 5; Leiden: E. J. Brill, 1974), 81–82.
15 The family resemblance between the ritual prescribed in Lev. 16:1–34 and the Lukan version of the story about the man possessed by legion (Lk. 8:26–39) is developed in fuller detail in Klutz, *The Exorcism Stories in Luke-Acts*, 144–48. Even stronger resemblance between the Leviticus ritual and the Synoptic story, with special focus on the Markan version (Mk 5:1–20), is argued by H. M. Moscicke, 'The Gerasene Exorcism and Jesus' Eschatological Expulsion of Cosmic Powers: Echoes of Second Temple Scapegoat Traditions in Mark 5.1–20', *JSNT* 41.3 (2019): 363–83.
16 Some measure of faith in Jesus can be inferred from the Markan portrayals of the Syrophoenician mother (Mk 7:25–30) and of the father whose son could not be healed by Jesus' disciples (Mk 9:19–29); but in neither of those instances is the possessed daughter/son described as exemplifying faith.
17 See especially John 6:60–71 and 12:4–8.
18 Enters and exits: 12:4–8; 13:26–31; 18:2–6. Mentioned in the discourses of Jesus: 6:64–71; 13:10–11; 17:13.
19 Mt. 8:16 (par. Mk 1:34); 8:31; 9:34; 12:24, 27, 28 (par. Mk 3:22; Lk. 11:14, 15, 18, 19, 20); Mk 1:39; 7:26; Lk. 13:32. Of the seventy-four occurrences of ἐκβάλλω

in the NT, only six are in the passive voice; and of the several that pertain to exorcistic events, only John 12:31 and Mt. 9:33 have the verb in the passive. The causes and effects of this pattern of usage in John 12:31 are given no serious attention in the scholarly literature but deserve careful analysis, not least because the combination of the passive voice and agent-deletion strongly affects what sorts of inferences can be drawn about the factors determining the given process of expulsion. In general, and especially in comparison with the exorcistic references in the Synoptics, the presentation of causal forces in John 12:31 is indirect and ambiguous, qualities that cohere well with the subsequent narration of events culminating in the withdrawal of the possessed Judas (John 13:21–30). But almost as importantly, the same ambiguity significantly decreases the likelihood of either 12:31 or the larger scheme of which it is a part being misconstrued as a flouting of Jesus' utterance in John 6:37: '… anyone who comes to me I will never drive away' (τὸν ἐρχόμενον πρὸς ἐμὲ οὐ μὴ ἐκβάλω ἔξω). As a result, the Johannine scheme offers a comparatively rich and complicated picture of the determining factors at play in the expulsion of the ruler, a process conceptualised as involving the participation not only of Jesus – e.g., his giving of the morsel, his command, his prior predictions – but also of Ps 41:10 (understood as prophetic in John 13:18), the satanic ruler himself, even Judas as his container, the departure of the latter being conceptualised in John 13:30 (ἐξῆλθεν) as an instance of what Lakoff and Johnson, *Philosophy in the Flesh*, 187, describe as a 'self-propelled movement'. That same movement strikingly resembles a different instance of departure, described in 1 John 2:19 as initiated by former members of the Christ association(s) assumed in various parts of the Johannine letters (1–3 John), on which see Martin, *Judas and the Rhetoric of Comparison*, 1–2, 132–33, 144–45.

20 Cf. Lincoln, *The Gospel according to St John*, 380.
21 Since the analysis above entails that the expulsion of Judas/RW is prefigured in John 12:7 and predicted in 12:31b, the representation of the denouement in 13:27–30 is richer and more complicated than either Beasley-Murray, *John*, 238–39, and Carson, *The Gospel according to John*, 474–75, or their exegetical adversaries (e.g., Wrede, Becker et al. who have inferred either a Satanic sacrament or a Judas without agency) imagine; for the relevant prophetic anticipations in John 12:7–13:26 preclude any notion of Judas seriously deliberating his options in 13:27–30, while the richness and multiplicity of determining factors in Judas' departure militate against any generalising reduction of the causation to 'magic'.
22 Vv. 26², 27, and 30.
23 ἄρτος (v. 18), δεῖπνον (vv. 2, 4), ἀνάκειμαι (vv. 23, 28), τρώγω (v. 18), ἑορτὴ (vv. 1, 29), and πάσχα (vv. 1, 28).
24 In a second century BCE inscription (*1PTebt* 33 rp.1) the diminutive form is used to designate small bits of food utilised for the purpose of luring a crocodile into a labyrinth. Similarly, but much later (8th c. CE), the diminutive is used in *PApoll* 001, 18 r.3 to refer to fragments of food used as bait in fishing. And the same form is used with the genitive of content φακοῦ in an early third-century CE inscription (*3PLond* 944.1) to signify a small cake of lentils. The term's wide range of referents, therefore, gives occasion for caution against assuming that the substance of the food in any given context is bread; but given the prominence of bread as a motif in John 6 and its occurrence in the immediately preceding co-text (13:18) of our passage, bread is probably to be understood as the substance of the morsel in John 13:26–30.
25 Especially after the dense recurrence of ἄρτος in John 6 and its use in 13:18.

26 Jd. 19:5 (B, a); Ru 2:14; 1 Sam. 28:22; 1 Kgs 17:11; Job 22:7; 24:10 (B, a); 31:17; Ps. 147:6 (17); Pr. 9:13; 17:1; 23:7; 28:21. The same term is also attested in the translations of Lev. 2:6 by Aquila, Symmachus, and Theodotion, the referent in that context being unleavened wafers broken in pieces and mixed with oil for presentation as a grain offering; see E. Hatch and H. Redpath, *A Concordance to the Septuagint and the Other Greek Versions of the Old Testament (Including the Apocryphal Books)*, vol. II (Oxford: Clarendon Press, 1897), 1490.
27 Part of the story about Saul (1 Sam. 28:23) is identified by the editors of the Nestle-Aland *Novum Testamentum Graece*, 28th edn (Stuttgart: Deutsche Bibelgesellschaft, 2012), 289, as an echo in Lk. 24:29, which is part of a meal story (Lk. 24:28–35) that may have been used in the composition of John 13. 1 Samuel 28 is remembered in full and rewritten in Josephus, *Ant*. 6.327–350; perhaps around the same time, and in abbreviated form, in *Pseudo-Philo* 64; and approximately a millennium later (c. 9th–12th centuries CE) in the *Palaea Historica* 151.7–15.
28 Judas in John 6:70 and 13:2; and Saul in 1 Sam. 16:14–23; 18:10; and 19:9.
29 Judas against Jesus in John 13:2, 21–30; and 18:1–11. Saul against David in 1 Sam. 18:6 – 19:17; 20:30–42; 23:6 – 24:7; 26:1–5; and 27:1–4.
30 As the prophet Samuel explains to Saul, the kingdom has been torn out of Saul's hand and given to David (1 Sam. 28:17); and as discussed below in connection with John 18, Judas' post-expulsion placement of himself close to the Roman detachment and the Judean police during the arrest of Jesus (18:5) is indicative of his ideological loyalties, especially in a context where Jesus goes on to define his kingdom as significantly different from those familiar to Pilate (18:33–38).
31 B. J. Malina, 'Feast', in *Biblical Social Values and Their Meaning*, ed. B. J. Malina and J. Pilch (Peabody, MA: Hendrickson, 1993), 76–77.
32 The suggestion offered here about the morsel coheres with a comparative consideration not yet mentioned: namely, although several features of John 13 possess eucharistic overtones (e.g., the bread mentioned in v. 18, and the taking and giving in v. 26), the larger narrative of the meal lacks a key term both relevant to the solidarity theme and present in all the institution and other eucharistic passages in the NT. The term is κλάω, used in fourteen of its fifteen occurrences in the NT to designate the eucharistic process of breaking shared bread; see esp. Mt. 26:26 (par. Mk 14:22; Lk. 22:19); and 1 Cor. 11:24. Also missing from the Johannine account, notably, is the verb εὐχαριστέω, whose absence is perhaps best explained in terms of its connotative dissonance with the immediately ensuing actions of Satan (v. 27) and Judas (v. 30). Thyen, *Das Johannes-evangelium*, 600–603, effectively summarises the case for interpreting the meal in John 13 as eucharistic but offers no comment on the absence of the lexemes just noted, a silence paralleled in most modern commentaries; see, e.g., Wengst, *Das Johannes-evangelium*, 113–15; and Brown, *John XIII–XXI*, 575–79.
33 Mt. 8:30–32; par. Mk 5:10–13; Lk. 8:31–33.
34 *T. Sol.* 5.11–12 (water); 6.10 (saffron); 16.7 (bowl); 18.20 (coriander); 18.31 (pure wine); 18.34 (olive oil); *The Bentresh Stela*, lines 19–24 (*ANET*, p. 30, foodstuffs for a festive meal). Although the origins and date of the *Testament of Solomon* in its long forms continue to be debated, the text's eighteenth chapter is based on source material that may have been produced in Hellenistic Egypt; and the references above to chapters 5, 6, and 16, occurring as they do in the text's first eighteen chapters, belong to an early redaction that I have dated to c. 75–175 CE. *The Bentresh Stela* is widely understood to have been produced in

either the Persian or the Ptolemaic period. On the dating of sources and redactional layers in the *Testament of Solomon*, see T. Klutz, *Rewriting the Testament of Solomon*, LSTS 53 (London: T & T Clark, 2005), 108–109, 131–33; and P. Busch, *Das Testament Salomos: Die älteste christliche Dämonologie, kommentiert und in deutscher Erstübersetzung*, TU 153 (Berlin: Walter de Gruyter, 2006), 233. On scholarly dating of *The Bentresh Stela*, see S. N. Morschauser, 'Using History: Reflections on the Bentresh Stela', *Studien zur Altägyptischen Kultur* 15 (1988): 203.

35 Flav. Josephus, *Ant.* 8.45–48 (finger-ring, root, water-pot); *Pes. K.* 4.7 (ashes from a red cow); *Arslan Tash No. 1* (7th c. BCE Phoenician amulet against child-killing demons); *T. Sol.* 22.9–20 (leather flask); Philostr., *VA* 3.38 (uncanny epistle); 4.10 (stones); 4.20 (statue); Acts 19:11–12 (clothing).

36 Cf. Kobel, *Dining with John*, 249–50. As noted by BDF §451, the conjunction οὖν does not always instantiate a causal connection but, especially after parenthetical elements (e.g., John 13:28–29), can be used with a loosely temporal nuance to resume the main plot of narrated actions. Since that type of meaning is very appropriate in John 13:30, the conjunction by itself should not be read as implying that either the command issued by Jesus in v. 27 or Judas' taking of the morsel directly caused the action of Judas' departure (v. 30). However, because the conceptual metaphor that sees causal priority as temporal priority is an essential part of the folk-theory of causation assumed in most forms of storytelling and narrative discourse, the temporal relations between the events narrated in John 13:26–30 invite the inference that Jesus' giving of the morsel (v. 26), Satan's entry into Judas' (v. 27), Jesus' command (v. 27), and Judas' taking of the morsel (v. 30) are all pieces of the causal puzzle presented by the account of Judas' exit in the context of John 13:30. On the conceptualisation of causal priority as temporal priority, and on the role of conceptual metaphors in theories of causation more generally, see Lakoff and Johnson, *Philosophy in the Flesh*, 221–27.

37 E.g., the 'experiential distance' between an academic conversation about the history of particle physics and the outdoor dining processes within which the conversation is taking place is much greater than the experiential distance between playing pickup basketball in the park and continuously trash-talking to your opponents (as some people do) while the game is in progress. On the concept of experiential distance in systemic functional linguistic approaches to register, see S. Eggins, *An Introduction to Systemic Functional Linguistics* (London: Pinter Publishers, 1994), 91–100.

38 Approximately the same measure of experiential distance continues without interruption into John 13:36–38.

39 Comparative evidence and other forms of support for this claim are discussed at length in chapter four of the present study.

40 Brown, *John XIII–XXI*, 558–59.

41 Martin, *Judas and the Rhetoric of Comparison*, 148–49.

42 Cf. Moloney, *Glory not Dishonor*, 20–22.

43 Cf. Martin, *Judas and the Rhetoric of Comparison*, 148 n. 43.

44 Faith alone is defended by Lincoln, *The Gospel according to St John*, 370, as the right idea; whereas Barrett, *The Gospel according to St John*, 441–42, infers baptism, understood as deriving its efficacy 'not through the *opus operatum* but from the word spoken' (John 15:3). Faith is certainly the more prominent theme in the wider literary co-text of the Fourth Gospel as a whole, but the possibility of double-symbolism in John 13:10 should not be ruled out.

45 Indeed, since the ψωμίον ('morsel') is best understood as a small fragment of the ἄρτος ('bread') mentioned by Jesus in 13:19, it is an example of 'symbolic

synecdoche, a phenomenon described by Lakoff and Johnson, *Metaphors We Live By*, 40, as particularly well-attested across a wide range of religious discourses.
46 Anticipated by Jesus in John 17:12 but never narrated as part of the plot of the Fourth Gospel.
47 Cf. Martin, *Judas and the Rhetoric of Comparison*, 148.
48 The present tense-form and imperfective aspect of ἔρχεται ('is coming') in John 14:30, whilst not unusual or marked in this context, deserves comment here both because it presents the action as incomplete at the moment of Jesus' utterance – a process of return, of coming back, has been initiated but is not yet finished, a description that would have made little or no sense prior to the withdrawal in 13:30 – and because the end of that process is highlighted by the Gospel narrator's use of the same form in 18:3, with ὁ Ἰούδας as the grammatical subject of ἔρχεται, to present Judas' arrival for the arrest of Jesus in the garden. At 18:3 the NRSV's 'So Judas brought a detachment of soldiers … and they came there with lanterns and torches and weapons' fails to indicate either the historic-present usage of the verb, its contribution to the cohesive tie back to 14:30, or the dependence of the participle λαβὼν on ἔρχεται as the sentence's main verb. The contribution of that same occurrence of ἔρχεται to both a lexical string and a reference chain between 18:3 and 14:30 is overlooked by most commentators including, e.g., Thyen, *Das Johannesevangelium*, 707–708; Beasley-Murray, *John*, 321–22; and Carson, *The Gospel according to John*, 577.
49 The key complex εἱστήκει δὲ καὶ Ἰούδας ὁ παραδιδοὺς αὐτὸν μετ' αὐτῶν ('And Judas, the one that betrayed him, was stood with them [i.e., with the Roman soldiers and Judean police]', 18:5) is the first of eleven instances between John 18:5 and 21:4 where the verb ἵστημι is used; and specifically in 18:5, but also in several other passages of the Gospel, the verb is used in a metaphorically extended sense, whereby select characters in the story are represented as taking up positions in physical or social space that indicate their relative proximity to Jesus in terms of loyalty. Judas' position of standing with the Roman soldiers and Judean police (18:5) during their exchange with Jesus implies his alliance with both sets of authorities against Jesus. Shortly afterwards the verb is used four times in descriptions of Peter as standing in positions that are comparatively more distanced than necessary from Jesus (18:16, 18^2, 25), leading directly to his third denial and the crowing of the cock (18:25–27). And in 19:25 and 20:11 Mary the mother of Jesus, Mary Magdalene, and other faithful women are portrayed as standing in places – either near the cross or at the tomb – whose physical nearness to places associated with Jesus is indicative of the women's loyalty to him. On metaphorical uses of ἵστημι, see LSJ, s.v., whose example from Xen., *HG* V.2.23 is semantically close to John 18:5 in particular; see also Hdt. 9.21; Eurip., *IT* 962. Representations of space are given similar attention by Neyrey, *The Gospel of John*, 58, 84, as part of a larger interest in territoriality in the Fourth Gospel, but are not probed for their potential significance specifically in John 18:5. For additional comment on the symbolic meaning of space in chapters 13, 18, and 21 of the Fourth Gospel, see Martin, *Judas' and the Rhetoric of Comparison*, 127–28.
50 See, e.g., John 3:19–21; and 12:46.
51 Thus, against Wright and Davies, 'John, Jesus, and "The Ruler of This World"', 76–78, neither a complete nor even a partial identification of 'the ruler of this world' and Caesar coheres with the portrayal of Judas/RW, the Roman soldiers, and the Judean police in John 18:3–5; but where Wright and

Davies nuance their interpretation by inferring 'a close alliance' of imperial power and satanic force (id., p. 81), their reading of the Gospel's outlook diverges less in substance than in emphasis from that suggested here.
52 After the reference in John 13:27 to Satan's entry into Judas, neither the narrator nor any other voice in John's Gospel ever suggests that Satan eventually vacates Judas; and the strong potential of Judas' arrival at the garden in John 18:3 to be read as a fulfilment of Jesus' word in 14:30 about the coming of the ruler reinforces the impression that Satan remains inside Judas to the very end of the Gospel.
53 Cf. R. Griffith-Jones, 'Apocalyptic Mystagogy: Rebirth-from Above in the Reception of John's Gospel', in *John's Gospel and Intimations of Apocalyptic*, ed. Williams and Rowland, 283–84.
54 As is widely overlooked, other than John 18:6 the only context in the Fourth Gospel where the syntagm ἀπῆλθον εἰς τὰ ὀπίσω ('they turned back') occurs is in the brief narration of certain unbelieving disciples withdrawing from Jesus (6:66), a note sandwiched closely by the Gospel's first two references to Judas, initially as betrayer (6:64) and next as διάβολος (6:70). With the presence of Judas thus being highlighted in the settings of both 6:64–70 and 18:1–6, the occurrence of ἀπῆλθον εἰς τὰ ὀπίσω in both passages has the effect of an *inclusio* for the Johannine story of Judas.
55 For the suggestion above, I am indebted to my University of Manchester colleague, G. J. Brooke, whose response to an early draft of the present study alerted me to the verticality overtones present in John 18:6. For ancient occurrences of πίπτω with connotations of defeat/failure, see LSJ, s.v. 'πίπτω'.
56 I.e., in John 12:31 and 13:30; and probably also, as discussed below, in 15:6.
57 Pss 19 (20):8; 26 (27):2; 81 (82):7; and 90 (91):7.
58 See G. Bohak, *Ancient Jewish Magic: A History* (Cambridge: Cambridge University Press, 2008), 108–110, 212–13, 379–80; and Klutz, *The Exorcism Stories in Luke-Acts*, 254–57.
59 Additional motifs contributing to the intertextual potential of LXX Psalm 90 and John 18:2–11 in its literary co-text include the close association of the demonic with darkness/night (LXX Ps. 90:5–6; John 13:27–32); the granting of 'glory' to the divinely protected (LXX Ps. 90:15; John 13:31–32); and the presence of God in the midst of affliction (LXX Ps. 90:15; John 17:11b–15; 18:4–11).
60 The body in 1 Cor. 11:29 being that of the Lord, as it explicitly is in 11:27, and thus not the congregation; cf. A. C. Thiselton, *The First Epistle to the Corinthians*, NIGTC (Grand Rapids: William B. Eerdmans, 2000), 890. The potential relevance of 1 Cor. 11:29 to understanding the morsel in John 13:26–30 is not the question addressed by D. B. Martin's comparative study of Paul's eucharistic assumptions and Graeco-Roman medical concepts of the *pharmakon* (Greek noun often meaning either 'medicine' or 'poison'); but the similarities highlighted by Martin between the eucharistic concept in 1 Cor. 11:17–34 and the *pharmakon* warrant an extension of his analysis to include the conceptualisation of the morsel in John 13:26–30, the most significant similarity for the present inquiry being that both Paul's eucharist and the *pharmakon* are 'ambiguous, dual-functioning' agents that could 'either kill you or cure you' depending on your state of being at the time of ingestion. See D. B. Martin, *The Corinthian Body* (New Haven: Yale University Press, 1995), 190–194, 196–97. The circulation and availability of these ideas not only among elite medical writers and professional practitioners but also in folk medicine, magico-ritual practice, and the eucharistic ideas of Paul entail that the cultural resources deployed in John 13:26–30 could easily have been

multiple and do not require a direct connection between the Fourth Gospel and 1 Corinthians in particular.

61 Carson, *The Gospel according to John*, 474–75, for instance, instead of exploring the implications of Jesus' command being addressed to a character possessed by Satan, argues against any presence of 'magic' in this setting and judges 'the gentleness and courtesy' attributed to Jesus in this verse as having the greater importance to its interpretation.

62 Both here and in my comments on John 15:1–8, I am indebted to David Ford's recent appropriation of research by Chrys Caragounis on semantic change prior to the NT era in the field of viticultural terms used in the present passage. Both Ford and Caragounis understand ἄμπελος in this context as signifying not a vine but rather a vineyard, with κλῆμα bearing the sense of 'vine' (i.e., the entire plant) rather than '(vine-)branch'; the resultant metaphors are Jesus as the vineyard, and his followers as the vines. See D. F. Ford, *The Gospel of John: A Theological Commentary* (Grand Rapids, MI, Baker Academic, 2021), 290–91, citing C. Caragounis, '"Abide in Me": The New Mode of Relationship between Jesus and His Followers as a Basis for Christian Ethics (John 15)', in *Rethinking the Ethics of John: "Implicit Ethics" in the Johannine Writings*, ed. J. G. van der Watt and R. Zimmermann (WUNT 291; Tübingen: Mohr Siebeck, 2012), 254.

63 See, e.g., Ford, *The Gospel of John*, 294; Thyen, *Das Johannes-evangelium*, 642; and Barrett, *The Gospel according to St John*, 474.

64 Thyen, *Das Johannes-evangelium*, 642, for instance, sees nothing worthy of note about Judas in the purity string; whereas Martin, *Judas and the Rhetoric of Comparison*, 126, perceptively interprets the same link as comparing Judas to the cleansed/pruned vine 'whose absence, caused by the cleansing/pruning power of Jesus' word', makes the remaining vines clean.

65 As, e.g., in Barrett, *The Gospel according to St John*, 474; and Carson, *The Gospel according to John*, 515, and especially well attested in occurrences of the singular forms of λόγος in the Gospel (e.g., 2:22; 4:41; 5:24, 38; 8:31, 37, 43, 51, 52, 55; 10:35; 12:48; 14:23; 15:20; 17:14).

66 Cf. Martin, *Judas and the Rhetoric of Comparison*, 126.

67 The idea of Jesus' word having a cleansing effect, as implied in John 15:3 and perhaps also intended in 13:27, is fully consonant with evidence offered above in my reading of the footwashing account as a field of metaphors for conceptualising a process of purification achieved through the exorcistic relocation of Judas, with the water used in the physical washing by Jesus being a symbol of the word of command uttered by Jesus in 13:27. A similar blend of concepts is attested in Eph. 5:26, where Christ is described as 'cleansing' his metaphorical bride 'with the washing of water by the word'.

68 See, e.g., Mt. 5:32 (par. Mk 5:13; Lk. 8:33); Mt. 12:43–44 (par. Lk. 11:24); Mt. 17:18 (par. Mk 9:26); Mk 1:25–26 (par. Lk. 4:35–36); Mk 5:8 (par. Lk. 8:29); Mk 7:29–30; and Acts 8:7; 16:18.

69 On the origins, development, and constitutive maxims of Grice's co-operative principle, see S. C. Levinson, *Pragmatics*, Cambridge Textbooks in Linguistics (Cambridge: Cambridge University Press, 1983), 100–118.

70 I.e., John 13:14–15 (by way of symbolic anticipation); 13:30–31; and 15:2–3, 6.

71 See the discussion and the sources cited in Klutz, *The Exorcism Stories in Luke-Acts*, 243–44.

4 Disorder, Discipline, and Eucharist in John 6–13

From Covert Infidelity to Overt Insult: Judas in John 6 and 12

The preceding chapters have focused chiefly on literary and linguistic aspects of key passages in the Fourth Gospel and select comparative texts. But neither linguistic criticism nor any other approach to exegesis can hope to provide a satisfying interpretation of a text without considering wider contextual factors that inform the text's production, reception, and potential relevance. The present chapter argues that one set of factors vital for optimal contextualisation of John 12:31, 13:1–30, and related parts of their co-text is the growing body of scholarly knowledge about association banqueting events in the social world of early Christ followers. As detailed below, insights from that area of study have potential to illuminate the Lord's Supper not only in the context of John 13 but also as it was practised in various settings across the next several centuries.

In the last few decades scholarship on Jewish synagogues and Christian assemblies in the Roman Empire has sought to understand the complexities of those groups as minority cultural collectives by comparing them not only with one another but also with a range of other groups such as occupational guilds, cult societies, philosophical clubs, and ethnically or geographically based associations.[1] Despite their diversity, and as Philip A. Harland has explained, the similarities now widely recognised between these groups warrants the description of all of them as 'associations' in a broad sense.[2] That shared description is based largely on evidence of a common interest attested across different groups in holding regular meetings for communal meals, for honouring patron deities and human benefactors of the group, for the pleasures of socialising with other members and having a positive sense of belonging to the group, and for purposes of ensuring good order on the part of members and dealing with any instances of offensive behaviour at dining events.[3]

As discussed below, all of those functions of association meals in the Graeco-Roman world can be seen as operative in varying degrees within

DOI: 10.4324/9781003359319-4

the inscribed setting of John 13; but while the meal narrated in John 13 has been recognised by several scholarly studies as an example of the common Graeco-Roman association banquet, with a supper proper followed by a symposium (e.g., philosophical discourse on an appropriate topic),[4] comparative study of the Johannine meal and analogous banquet traditions has thus far not significantly enriched scholarly interpretation of either the withdrawal/expulsion of Judas or any of the processes closely related to it in the Fourth Gospel.[5] The ensuing comments are thus offered to the general end of providing the desired enrichment, but also more specifically to demonstrate that both the utterance of Jesus in John 12:31 and much of his behaviour as narrated in John 13:1–30 acquire a rich but largely overlooked additional layer of meaning when they are recognised as an attempt by Jesus, as the leader of an emergent cult association, to resolve a problem of group order occasioned by offensive behaviour on the part of one member towards several others.

The problem posed by Judas for the Jesus circle in the Fourth Gospel has been mentioned in various connections above but has not been given focussed attention from the comparative standpoint of good order and discipline at association meals. The relevance of order and discipline to the relationship between the Jesus circle and Judas becomes partly evident in the account of the controversy over Jesus' bread-of-life discourse (John 6:25–59), where Jesus is characterised as knowing that Judas not only was aligned with a group of disciples who could not accept Jesus' teaching in that context (6:60–66) but also 'was the one that would betray him' (6:64). When the disputation erupts over Jesus' teaching in this setting, Jesus and his disciples are in the process of becoming a distinct group, an embryonic association whose boundaries and identity are made clearer by the teaching and controversy in 6:25–71. Judas, however, in contrast to those unnamed disciples offended by Jesus' bread-of-life teaching (6:66), does not distance himself physically from Jesus at this point (6:66) but instead stays on as a member of the chosen twelve and continues to meet with the group;[6] and since the particular teaching that Judas cannot accept is strongly fused to the immediately preceding narration of Jesus' superabundant provision of food through his multiplication of loaves and fishes (6:1–15) – of which Judas, as one of the twelve, was surely a beneficiary (6:3, 12) – the blend of unbelief, ingratitude, and enmity attributed to Judas towards Jesus in the ensuing interpretation of the controversy (6:60–71) might seem to constitute grounds for disciplinary action or even permanent exclusion from the group.

At no point in John 6, however, is the possibility of Judas being penalised even hinted; and when the presentation of Judas in John 6:60–71 is read in the light of ancient comparative sources regarding improprieties at association meetings and how they should be handled, the absence of any disciplinary response to Judas' disposition in John 6 becomes readily intelligible. For starters, the defects attributed to Judas in the context of John 6:60–71 are focalised only through the consciousnesses of Jesus and the narrator, and thus are far from being publicly recognised at that point in the plot; indeed, since Judas is not presented in that context as engaging in any form of material action or even as speaking, he cannot properly be understood by that point in the Gospel as having committed a wrongdoing that could be attested by witnesses in the context of reference. As discussed below, the importance of witnesses and public perception in situations of in-group disputation more generally is known to have been a matter of interest to ancient associations and therefore helps to explain the absence of group intervention regarding Judas in John 6.

Between the bread-of-life controversy in John 6 and the beginning of the meal in John 13, however, the tenor of Judas' interactions with Jesus himself and other Christ followers changes in ways that have significant consequences for interpreting John 13:1–30. In the narrative about the meal in Bethany at the home of Lazarus with his sisters Mary and Martha (John 12:1–8), Jesus' recent 'sign' of raising Lazarus from the dead (11:1–44) is presented summarily as part of the orientation to the complicating actions that directly follow in the same dinner episode (12:1); and since the narrator explicitly indicates that the dinner was given for Jesus (12:2), the nature of the meal as an act of reciprocity and gratitude for the prior restoration of Lazarus to his family is clear. Moreover, from the perspective of recent theories that highlight the role of religious ritual in 'costly signalling',[7] Mary's action of anointing Jesus' feet with expensive perfume not only contributes to the family's efforts to honour Jesus but also signals a willingness to incur significant costs for the sake of continuing the flow of cooperative exchange with him. But most importantly, since the overall cost of the perfume and dinner is at least an approximate indication of how very highly the family esteems both Jesus himself and the value of Lazarus's restored life, the negative honour-challenge implicit in Judas' subsequent question – 'Why was this perfume not sold for three hundred denarii and the money given to the poor?' (12:5) – has remarkable potential to offend every other named participant in the episode:[8] Jesus, for instance, is implied to have done nothing worthy of Mary's costly gesture and to be no higher than Judas himself in the ranks of honour and status – hence Judas regards himself as worthy of challenging Jesus in the presence of others; simultaneously, Mary is criticised as having overestimated both the social worth of Jesus in general and the value of his prior restoration of Lazarus in particular; the life of Lazarus, by extension, is likewise demeaned; and through the logic of kinship and family honour, Mary's sister Martha also is insulted and her table service devalued.

Additionally, since the Johannine Jesus is the head of the given group and thus embodies its collective honour,[9] Judas' challenge is indicative of his disregard for the group as a whole; and in stark contrast to Mary's gesture with the perfume, the challenge communicated by Judas serves to signal neither an interest in cooperating with the group nor a willingness to make costly sacrifices for its reputation and survival. But most significant for the present analysis, by the end of the meal narrated in John 12:1–8, Judas' uncooperative and insulting behaviour are no longer largely private but now – in contrast to the circumstances portrayed back in John 6:60–71 – are semi-public and potentially known to at least three members of the Christ group in addition to Jesus himself. As for the group's immediate response to Judas, the silence of Mary in particular is entirely consistent with the male-orientated system of honour and shame in the ancient Mediterranean context of culture but also, in terms of the values of that same system, an example of respectable female behaviour; whereas Jesus' pragmatically direct riposte ('Leave her alone', 12:7) is typical of how an honourable male in the same milieu is expected to defend the honour of the females in his circle of family and friends.[10] Significantly, the same riposte demonstrates the Johannine Jesus' willingness and ability to deal firmly with insulting behaviour within the group, qualities he will display yet again, subtly but effectively, in John 13:1–30.

Cumulatively, all the observations just given help to set the stage for an interpretative scenario consonant with other levels of analysis in the sections above but significantly different from the prevailing scholarly readings of John 13:1–30 and its literary co-text. In the interest of properly developing a new and better scenario, at least brief consideration needs to be focused on how the behaviour attributed to Judas in the meal episode just discussed (John 12:1–8) might have been perceived and handled by various associations in the same broad sociocultural milieu in which the Fourth Gospel was produced.

Banquets and Association Order in the Social World of John 12–13

The Qumran Cave 1 manuscript of the Community Rule (1QS), long understood by experts on the Dead Sea Scrolls as serving to define the Qumran community, includes three columns of text (5–7) devoted to matters of group discipline, including the behaviour of members during meetings.[11] In particular, members are enjoined to meet together regularly in groups of ten for meals (6:2–3); grievances are not to be raised by one member of the community against another 'unless it is with reproof in the presence of witnesses' (6:1); and the prescribed penalties for wrongdoing vary in accordance with the severity of the transgression, ranging from brief periods of exclusion from the community (e.g., ten days for falling asleep during a meeting, 7:11) to lengthier periods of banishment for intentionally insulting another member without just cause (7:4–5), and outright expulsion for defaming the community more generally (7:16–17). On the whole, these clauses and others like them in the same manuscript closely resemble the idealised portrayal of the Second Temple Jewish association identified as the Essenes in Flavius Josephus *War* 2.119–161, in which the Essene group's exemplary carefulness in deciding cases of community discipline is underscored (*War* 2.145), and where the penalty imposed on the group's most serious offenders is described in terms strikingly similar to those used in the Johannine Jesus' prediction about the expulsion of Judas: namely, the Essenes expel (ἐκβάλλουσιν) such offenders from the community and thereby set 'the excriminated individual' (ὁ ἐκκριθείς) on a path that leads to a miserable end (*War* 2.143).[12]

Indirectly, the high value or even necessity of community rules like those just mentioned is attested in ancient sources regarding several other associations in the environment of the early Christians. For instance, in an idealised description of a broadly Essene-like but distinct subgroup of Jews known as the Therapeutae, the first-century CE Jewish Middle Platonist writer Philo of Alexandria (c. 20 BCE to 50 CE) highlights the moral excellence of that group and most especially the simplicity and conviviality of their common banquets (*Contempl.* 64–89). Philo produces the desired portrayal partly by contrasting the meetings of the Therapeutae sharply to the meal practices of various pagan associations (40–89). Regarding the pagan dining events, Philo singles out the frequent occurrence of insults, fighting, injuries, and generally violent behaviour, much of it being fuelled at table by insatiably greedy drinking of wine,[13] with murder and deaths only being prevented by the presence of an association officer tasked with umpiring the event. Like several other ancient sources that include critical comment on clubs and associations, Philo's treatment of these matters is widely understood to be a rhetorically motivated exaggeration of the culpabilities of the pagan associations and their banquets;[14] but underlying the rhetorical exaggeration, almost certainly, is a layer of social reality whose relevance for the present inquiry should not be passed over. Partly because of the generally status-orientated and agonistic character of ancient Mediterranean society, and perhaps also in some instances due to the widespread custom of copious wine-drinking at banquets, the potential for tension and conflicts to arise within association meetings must have become a reality at least occasionally;[15] otherwise, there would have been little or no need for rules such as those noted above. But most important for the present discussion, a similar kind of social reality is both assumed and implied in the portrayal of Judas and the Jesus circle in John 6:60–71; 12:31; and 13:1–30, where in-group grumbling and tensions at community meals set the stage for a member of the Jesus circle to go outside the group and eventually, it is implied, slander it before an audience of powerful out-group authorities (18:2–5).[16]

The Johannine characterisation of Judas as not merely leaving the last banquet early[17] but eventually going to out-group Judaean and Roman authorities and disclosing to them association confidences (18:1–5) is another feature of the Gospel story whose social significance can be illuminated by comparison with ancient sources regarding associations and their rules. Written only a few decades earlier than the Fourth Gospel, the apostle Paul's epistolary response to select moral improprieties in the Christ assembly at Corinth includes common association teaching that all in-group grievances be settled by adjudication strictly within the community, rather than taking the disputes to civic courts for judgement (1 Cor. 6:1). Strikingly, much like the implied author of John 13:26–30, in this same epistolary context the apostle conceptualises a given instance of insider wrongdoing as engaging the interest and involvement of Satan (1 Cor. 5:3–5), and as requiring exclusion from the congregation's fellowship meals (5:9–11), a judgement understood by Paul as entailing the offender's outright expulsion from the community (5:13). But finally, in addition to those similarities a significant contrast between the Fourth Gospel and 1 Corinthians is to be observed in connection with the airing of in-group grievances before out-group unbelieving authorities: namely, in 1 Corinthians it is not the individual wrongdoer but rather the community as a whole that is reproved by Paul for in-group disputes being tried 'before the unrighteous' (6:6); whereas in the Fourth Gospel it is not the Jesus circle as a whole but rather Judas alone who is presented as culpable, albeit only implicitly, for the eventual involvement of Judaean and Roman outsiders against Jesus (John 18:2–5). This particular infraction on Judas' part, moreover, should probably be understood in John, as also in Luke (22:3–6), to be essential to what is intended by the description of Judas as the one who 'betrayed' Jesus, the gospel discourse of betrayal having now been illuminated by our awareness of the common association rule against disclosing in-group grievances or other risky information to persons outside the group.[18] But more importantly, awareness of the aforementioned contrast between the Fourth Gospel and 1 Corinthians has potential to deepen our sense of Judas' wickedness, of his disloyalty to the Jesus group and its leader, and of the appropriateness of association discipline (e.g., expulsion from the group) therefore being applied in his case.[19]

In both the Johannine and the Pauline situations, the assumption that in-group conflicts should not be aired before outsiders but instead be managed within the circle is indicative of the high importance attached to group honour throughout the wider Mediterranean cultural context and has close analogues not only in the Community Rule text cited above but also in a second-third century CE inscription known as the 'Statutes of the Iobacchoi', a Greek text of 163 lines providing extensive detail about the organisational structure and regulations of an Athenian religious association devoted to Dionysus/Bakchos and active from around the middle of the second century.[20] Of the numerous regulations set forth in this inscription, those most pertinent to the present discussion are concerned with defining penalties for disorderly behaviour including verbal abuse of other members at a group banquet (73–83), taking in-group grievances after a banquet to public adjudicators rather than to the association priest (91–95), and failure on the part of 'the orderly officer' to eject members for fighting at a banquet (94–95). Cases of wrongdoing were to be settled, therefore, within the assembly and required testimony from at least two in-group witnesses (73–83), with penalties for proven misbehaviour ranging from light monetary fines (80–83) and temporary exclusion (84–95) to outright ejection (136–145). In that light, the type of behaviour exemplified by the Johannine Judas' implied referral of his complaint against the Jesus circle to out-group authorities (John 18:2–5) would most probably have smelled bad not only to the apostle Paul and the covenanters of Qumran but also to the Dionysiac producers of the Statutes of the Iobacchoi.

At least one other feature of the Johannine portrayal of Judas has potential to be illuminated by comparative analysis of the Iobacchoi inscription. As just noted, the statutes of the Iobacchoi assume the presence of a club 'orderly officer' (εὔκοσμος) responsible for ejecting any members who come to blows at meetings. The same role, described later in the inscription as a position of considerable honour (136–137), gives authority to the officeholder to identify any members guilty of disorderly conduct at gatherings for association meals (137–140). By exercising this authority, the orderly officer – also referred to as the 'rod-bearer' (ῥαβδοφορίας, 131), for reasons to be seen presently – helps the *archibakchos* (i.e., the group priest) to decide whether any member(s) should be excluded from the club banquet hall or, in cases of refusal to depart peaceably, be forcefully ejected (137–145). But for purposes of the present comparison, what is most noteworthy about this section of the association's rules is the procedure it prescribes for the orderly officer's identification of unruly members for possible exclusion: namely, he is to 'bear the wand [θύρσον] of the god'[21] to any disorderly participant and put it directly next to them during the banquet, a ritual-like action that communicates non-verbally to the attendant priest and his assistants that the participant in question may need to be removed (137–141). The orderly officer's use of the wand thus bears a remarkable resemblance to Jesus' use of the eucharistic morsel in John 13:24–30 to identify the wrongdoer who, immediately after receiving the item from Jesus, departs from the group.

The purpose of the foregoing comparison being strictly analogical rather than genealogical, the similarity between the morsel and the wand is highlighted here chiefly to reinforce my case for interpreting John 13:1–30 as the narration of an association banquet at which disciplinary action against an uncooperative member has become an urgent necessity in the eyes of the group leader.[22] That same disciplinary interpretation, however, should it be adopted, would have a couple of implications that are best mentioned here. First, it would entail that the oft-discussed ethical tension between radically inclusive love and sectarian exclusivity in scholarly interpretation of the Fourth Gospel needs to be rethought in the light of the Johannine Judas' eviction from the Jesus circle, an exclusionary process in which the agency of Jesus is presented not as antithetic to divine love but rather as required by it (e.g., for purposes of purifying and protecting the other disciples).[23] But second, and just as importantly, the disciplinary connotations inferred by the present study militate against the modern scholarly tradition of interpreting the Johannine Judas as representing the so-called 'secessionists', an assumed faction of former members of the Johannine community whose eventual departure from that group contributed to the agonistic context implied by some parts of the Fourth Gospel and 1 John;[24] for contrary to that reading, the present interpretation of Judas' removal in John 13:30 as an outcome of association discipline entails that, whilst Judas is portrayed in that context as exercising a certain limited form of agency, his departure from the group is neither entirely voluntary nor fuelled by disagreements over Christology or the eucharist. Instead, according to my proposed scenario of association discipline, Judas leaves the group because the Johannine Jesus has just behaved in multiple ways that effectively signal it is now time for Judas to depart; but in the event that Judas somehow fails to get Jesus' point, he would surely understand that the query initiated by Peter in the same setting, regarding the identity of the betrayer (13:34), probably arises less from epistemic curiosity than from the practical responsibilities of a typical association 'bouncer'.[25]

The functional similarity observed above between the wand and the morsel possesses an additional, secondary layer of meaning for the present investigation. By highlighting the morsel as an item of comparative significance, the interpretative process of inferring the resemblance has the effect of heightening the prominence attached to the morsel earlier in the present study based on the distinctively Johannine character of the noun ψωμίον and its repetition in 13:26-30. But in addition, since the form and usage of that term can be contextualised in relation to ancient Mediterranean banquets and their rules more fruitfully at this point in my inquiry than earlier, a couple of rarely asked questions about the morsel now seem ripe for attention.

The questions revolve around the significance of the implied size of the morsel on the one hand, and the timing of Jesus' introduction and handing of the morsel to Judas relative to the order of happenings in the larger *deipnon*-symposium sequence in John 13-17 on the other hand.

One of the main reasons these questions ought to be asked, moreover, is that although they might possess only modest or even no relevance to most meal settings familiar to readers of the present book, they implicate more general areas of symbolic action that are increasingly understood as having weighty significance for the relative honour-rankings of participants at meals both in the ancient world and in certain more recent contexts studied by anthropologists and ethnographers. As Dennis Smith and others have shown with reference to the Graeco-Roman context, both the size of the food portions served to diners at a given event and the order in which the diners are served relative to each other can carry a heavy load of social value and significance.[26] Inequalities in portion sizes and their presumed basis in status-based orders of distribution are interpreted convincingly by Smith as having particular relevance in the assumed situation of the aforementioned Iobacchoi rules.[27] Similar kinds of dining issues have been understood by some New Testament scholars as an important part of what the apostle Paul is challenging in 1 Cor. 11:17–34;[28] and nearly identical understandings of portion size and order of service at meals are discussed by anthropologist Bruce Kapferer in his outstanding study of demon ceremonies in modern Sri Lanka, where strong concern with status and the premium placed on hierarchy in Sinhalese culture are displayed in various aspects of exorcistic performance, and where exorcism and community dining are often integrated into a single complex ceremony.[29] In the light of those studies and others, the size of the morsel in John 13:26–30 and the relative timing of its provision to Judas deserves at minimum a brief rethinking.

As noted earlier regarding ψωμίον in John 13:26–30, the suffix ιον makes the nominal root diminutive in form and serves to represent the food item in that context as small.[30] Despite the diminutive morphology, scholarly commentaries and translations tend on the whole to read the noun in John as if its meaning were indistinguishable from that of the masculine cognate ψωμός;[31] and thus, in English, renderings such as 'piece of bread' (NRSV) and 'sop' (KJV) are not uncommon. Greater awareness of the distinctive potential of the diminutive is shown by the English Standard Version's use of 'morsel'. In terms of a critical practice such as George Steiner's translation hermeneutics, the difficulty posed by ψωμίον in this context involves not only 'embodiment' – finding the best word or phrase in the target language ('piece of bread', 'morsel', 'crumb' etc.) – but also 'penetration', the task of analysing the source text deeply enough to discover its alien particularity or otherness.[32] In regard to the usage and effects of ψωμίον in John 13:26–30, the potential for deeper invasion might begin to be realised by asking how the repetition of the diminutive in the given passage is likely to have been heard by early audiences who knew from first-hand dining experience the significance of portion sizes for their own relative honour-ratings and social statuses. In the inscribed context of the meal in John 13, and especially with Jesus' provisions of food or drink at other points in the Gospel being marked by superabundance,[33] his passing of the significantly small morsel to Judas stands out by contrast to his other food-producing performances and has the effect of a symbolic action conveying a negative appraisal of Judas' status in the group.

Furthermore, in a context such as that sketched above regarding religious associations and their dining codes, the same negative challenge to Judas' honour should probably be understood as intensified by the timing of Jesus' gesture. More specifically, since the footwashing is presented as taking place during the meal (13:2) and the meal scene concludes with Judas taking the morsel from Jesus and departing (13:30), the giving and receiving of the morsel are presented as the final transaction involving food at the supper. Thus, in addition to being apportioned a demeaningly small bit of food, Judas is singled out in John 13:1–30 as the last diner at table to be served; and thereby the Johannine Jesus communicates yet another negative honour-challenge to Judas, less through verbal discourse than through ritual-symbolic action involving food.

Decisions about portion size and temporal priority at dinner are not the only processes through which Jesus conveys negative challenges to Judas' honour in John 13. For instance, since the idea of betraying Jesus is presented in John 13:2 as having entered Judas' heart before Jesus arises from the table in 13:4 to perform the footwashing, Judas can be expected to know who Jesus is referring to when he subsequently implies that at least one disciple at the meal is unclean (13:10). Because of the same sequence of events, the comparably negative challenges issued by Jesus to Judas in 13:18 and 21 - 'I am not speaking about all of you' (v. 18) and 'one of you will betray me' (v. 21) – are likewise best construed as being comprehended by their target, the only listener capable of knowing who Jesus is challenging through these utterances being Judas himself. Indeed, since the verbal exclusion of Judas in 13:18 is grounded in Jesus' knowledge that Judas will never rise to the ethical challenge implicit in the footwashing (vv. 12–17), the footwashing's clarification of the kinds of costly sacrifices required for true belonging to the Jesus circle – humility, and in-group love to the point of dying for the friends[34] – should perhaps be interpreted as contributing to Judas' expulsion. Instead of lowering the bar for Judas, the Johannine Jesus raises it; Judas, knowing the game is over, departs from the circle at last; and thereby a warning is conveyed to any group members whom the Johannine Judas-figure might symbolise – the unproductive vines of John 15:1–8, for instance, or free-riders and the generally uncooperative – in the implied situation of the Gospel's production. And finally, if we understand the behaviour of the Johannine Judas more generally as an effort to dishonour Jesus and thereby elevate his own honour-ranking through deceit and trickery, the supramundane knowledge implicit in the counter-challenges attributed to Jesus serves to demonstrate that it is not Jesus but rather Judas who turns out in the end to be tricked; for in a potent turn of dramatic irony, by acting in ways that result in his own expulsion from the Christ followers, the Johannine Judas ultimately succeeds only in co-facilitating the purification of the other disciples and heightening the glory of Jesus and his father (John 13:31-32).

So many negative challenges are therefore conveyed by Jesus to Judas in John 13:1-30 that it is difficult to escape the implication that Jesus' behaviour is consciously motivated by a desire to remove Judas from the group. Certainly, from a perspective informed by the banqueting customs and codes of behaviour discussed above, that sort of motivation would make appropriate sense as an association leader's response to the difficulties posed by the presence of an insulting, uncooperative, and dangerous diner at the meal. The same kind of drive would also give additional meaning and rationale to the exorcistic character of the action inferred in my reading of John 12:31 and 13:30 as the core of a literary-schematic structure: namely, the exorcism would constitute a creative but also culturally intelligible approach to the task of ousting Judas. And finally, the same intentionality on the part of the Johannine Jesus would result in an attractive dovetailing of what is clearly necessary for fulfilling the divine plan on the one hand – that is, Judas must eventually leave the group if he is to betray Jesus and set in motion the sequence of Jesus arrest and passion – and what is paradigmatically ethical for the Jesus' circle as an ancient Mediterranean religious association on the other hand: they must discipline and, wherever appropriate, be willing to expel uncooperative or hostile members from the group.[35] In brief, both the divine plan and association ethical norms require Judas to be cast out.

From Exorcistic Innovation to Apotropaic Analogues

Of the potentially many questions that could be raised in response to the contextualisation just proposed, only one can be given priority for discussion here. If we assume that the Johannine Jesus is intent, as just suggested, on removing Judas from the group, what kinds of considerations might help us to understand why Jesus would think that a specifically exorcistic method would be better suited to the task than either a strictly verbal, physically coercive, or other type of approach? The larger ritual frame of supper-symposium in which the proposed exorcistic performance would be embedded (John 13-17), including as it does the ritual-like action of the footwashing in 13:1-20, points to an answer worth considering. The high density and rich variety of ritual-symbolic forms and performative action in these chapters, and especially in John 13:1–30, may be indicative that both the subject matter and the issues at stake in the inscribed setting are too complicated, too risky and dangerous for the various identities involved, to be negotiated largely through the informalities of spontaneous verbal exchange.[36] A similar impression emerges at several points in the same section where speech and conversation are used by select characters in ways that are so indirect and ambiguous that the resultant confusion and uncertainties eventually emerge as a salient theme requiring interpretation in their own right. In the unit's first instance of embedded dialogue, for instance, where Jesus is asked whether he is going to wash Peter's feet (13:6), the first part of Jesus response is, 'You do not now know what I am doing' (13:7). Shortly afterwards in the same conversation, where Jesus tells Peter that not all of the disciples 'are clean' (13:10), neither Peter nor the other disciples at table (except for Judas himself) possess the knowledge shared by the implied author and audience that the unnamed embodiment of impurity is Judas.[37] A similar instance of ambiguity, again regarding Judas, follows when the imminent betrayal is mentioned by Jesus himself for the first time in the Gospel – 'one of you will betray me' (v. 21) – but without disclosing the name of the betrayer. The story's narrator, after going on to endorse the suggestion above regarding the uniquely disconcerting quality of the whole situation (v. 21), then proceeds to underscore the other disciples' lack of knowledge about Judas more generally by confirming that Jesus' ambiguity about the identity of the betrayer has the effect of prolonging the disciples' condition of unknowing: 'The disciples looked at one another, uncertain of whom he was speaking' (NRSV, v. 22). On the question at hand, both Peter and even the Beloved Disciple remain in the dark (vv. 23–25); and significantly, when the latter asks Jesus the question directly, 'Lord, who is it?' (v. 25), Jesus does not respond with a straight answer but instead indicates that the truth will be revealed through his giving of the morsel (v. 26). And finally, after Judas takes the morsel, the conspicuously imprecise command addressed by Jesus to Judas – 'Do quickly what you are about to do' (v. 27) – becomes a source of still further uncertainty for everyone else at table (vv. 28–29).

In the light of this protracted sequence of ambiguities, the Johannine Jesus' use of ritual forms such as the supper proper, the washing of the disciples' feet, and exorcism can be seen as a socially adept choice and combination of strategies for managing the situation at hand.[38] The pragmatic efficacy of that choice, and especially of the exorcistic performance, can be seen in the affective contrast between what precedes the exorcistic dénouement (v. 30) and what follows it: as soon as Judas' departure from the supper is narrated as the exorcistic climax (vv. 30–31), the immediately preceding flow of conversational opaqueness begins to recede, with Jesus' ensuing discourse of glory and love (vv. 31–35) being spoken in a style much clearer than that of his preceding comments about the footwashing and Judas. The existence of that same contrast, moreover, in so far as it is also a change that occurs across the time before Judas' departure to the period after it, contributes to a general resemblance between the phasing of exorcistic elements of vv. 1–30 and the classic triadic structure and phasing of exorcisms as theorised more generally by Bruce Kapferer.[39] The latter scheme, adapted by Kapferer from earlier influential work by Arnold van Gennep and Victor Turner,[40] sees exorcistic events as unfolding sequentially in three phases, namely:

1 *the separation phase*, a period in which the patient is detached from the mundane world of familiar social structures in preparation for a process of healing and transformation;
2 *the liminal phase*, a period in which the patient experiences ambiguity and disorientation, in a space where the assumed demonic and divine forces are elaborated and ritually joined in struggle by the human participants; and
3 *the reaggregation phase*, a period in which the demonic comes to be experienced as clearly subordinate to the divine, with the patient thus being freed from demonic affliction, given a new and better identity, and enabled to function in normal ways or even better.

From the perspective of that scheme, the beginning of a formal association-style supper whose participants include a figure now strongly under the influence of the devil (13:2) would mark the commencement of the *separation phase*, a stage continuing through the pre-conversational cycle of actions performed by Jesus – most notably, his standing up after the supper has begun (vv. 2–4), his disrobing (v. 4), and his washing of the disciples' feet (v. 5) – which cumulatively serve well to hint that the supper now in progress is going to differ in certain ways from other meals, including those narrated earlier in the Gospel. From the end of that phase, the stream of ambiguities and unanswered questions running from Peter's initial query about Jesus' actions (v. 6) up to and including Jesus' introduction of the morsel (v. 26) would constitute the *liminal phase*, in whose final moments the numinous quality of the morsel as food provided by Jesus strongly signals the possibility of the confusion and disturbance narrated directly beforehand being reversed and overcome. And finally, the realisation of the transformative potential of the food given by Jesus – indeed, the demonstration of that potential in both the relocating of the possessed Judas and the consequent glorification of God and 'the son of man' (vv. 30–32) – along with the additionally consequent re-orderings of social and cosmic space, would constitute Kapferer's *reaggregation phase*.

Disorder, Discipline, and Eucharist in John 6–13 73

The commensurability of Kapferer's model of exorcistic ceremonies on the one hand and the events narrated in John 13:1–30 on the other hand is scarcely adequate, either by itself or even in conjunction with other relevant evidence offered in the present study, for proving once and for all the exorcistic character of Jesus' interaction with Judas in the given context. The model should, however, be credited at minimum for strengthening the case for the existence of a significant family resemblance between the relevant events in John 12–13 and even a conventionally narrow definition of exorcism.

But just as important, if Jesus' introduction of the morsel in John 13:26–27 not only plays a key role in good community-housekeeping, similar to the wand of Dionysus,[41] and suggests the apotropaic power of the eucharist but also hints at the reversal about to occur in the reaggregation phase of the exorcism rite, the richness of the morsel's semantic potential in that setting constitutes an instance of conceptual blending whose full range of effects have perhaps never been adequately ascertained.[42] In addition to being distinctively polyvalent, the same instance of conceptual dexterity shows no evidence of having been received, in whole, from either Paul, the Synoptic Gospels, sources used by the Synoptics, or other Christ-group traditions potentially earlier than the composition of the Fourth Gospel. Accordingly, while fresh conceptual integrations are now widely understood to be produced by many human beings in the course of daily living, the particular integration just described stands out as so distinctive in the historical situation of the Fourth Gospel that it beckons a comparative quest for any similar blends attested from the Fourth Gospel's circulation and use in the first few centuries of the Common Era. From early in the second century CE to around the sixth or seventh century survives a range of comparative materials which, although they are not directly concerned with John 12:31 or 13:26–30, provide evidence that the distinctive integration of exorcism, apotropaic praxis, and the Christian eucharist in the Johannine context may have contributed significantly to subsequent Christian understandings of those types of processes.

Several of the letters attributed to Ignatius of Antioch, the early Christian bishop (c. 35–107), have been interpreted as showing knowledge of the Fourth Gospel,[43] a hypothesis recently adopted by G. Twelftree to explain a number of long-recognised affinities between the Gospel and the Ignatian corpus, including what Twelftree sees as a shared preference for non-exorcistic approaches to managing Satan and the demonic powers.[44] Twelftree's view of the matter, however, takes for granted a tightly bounded concept of exorcism that has little if any scope for extension on the basis of family resemblance,[45] and which therefore functions as a hindrance rather than an aid to comparative analysis of John 13:26–30 and anything in Ignatius that might significantly resemble it. As it happens,

Ignatius's letter to the Ephesians includes a passage of considerable comparative interest.

Following an exhortation enjoining his Christian audience to increase the frequency of their eucharistic celebrations,[46] Ignatius indicates his reason for the command: 'For when you frequently gather as a congregation, the powers of Satan are destroyed, and his destructive force is vanquished by the harmony of your faith' (Ign., *Eph.* 13.1). By conceptualising frequent and harmonious eucharistic celebrations as having power to defeat the forces of Satan, this brief passage instantiates a conceptual integration similar to that proposed above for John 13:30 but unattested in earlier Christ-group sources; but almost as importantly, since Ignatius specifies that the purpose of these meetings is not only for the eucharist but also for giving 'glory' (δόξα) to God, the eucharist-prophylaxis-Satan blend in this passage is collocated with δόξα in a manner that strongly resembles a combination of lexemes and motifs found together likewise in John 12:28–31 and 13:26–32. Although the relationship between the Johannine and Ignatian passages is too oblique to be seen as citational or deliberately allusive, at minimum it merits consideration as a possible echo of the Fourth Gospel in the Ignatian text and an early stage in the development of the eucharist-prophylaxis blend.

The anthological composition known as the *Gospel of Philip* survives only in the form of a single fourth- or fifth-century Coptic text preserved as the third tractate in Nag Hammadi Codex II (NHC II,3) and is generally assumed to be either a translation or a copy of a translation of a work originally composed in Greek but no longer extant and of uncertain provenance.[47] Two separate excerpts in this tractate are connected by lexical strings and shared concepts in a manner that has noteworthy consequences for the present inquiry. In the first excerpt of the two, *G. Phil.* 58.10–14, Jesus is the implied sayer of a short formal prayer introduced by the text's narrator and placed explicitly in a setting of eucharistic ritual – 'He [i.e., Jesus] said on that day in the Eucharist [ⲧⲉⲩⲭⲁⲣⲓⲥⲧⲉⲓⲁ]' – the words of the eucharistic prayer itself being: 'You have united perfect light with the Holy Spirit; unite the angels [ⲛⲁⲅⲅⲉⲗⲟⲥ] with us also, as images [ⲛ̄ϩⲓⲕⲱⲛ].'[48] Read in isolation of its literary co-text within *Philip*, nothing about Jesus' utterance just quoted would seem to involve impure spirits, exorcism, or protection against demonic attack; and interpretative efforts such as that by Lundhaug, to determine as much of the prayer's meaning as possible on the basis of the reference directly beforehand to Jesus' transfiguration (*G. Phil.* 57.28–58.9), give a very similar impression, in addition to creating a nest of exegetical difficulties that Lundhaug's own study leaves largely unresolved.[49] However, a significantly different impression of the prayer in *Philip* comes to the fore when the same excerpt is read in the light of another situated later in the tractate and flavoured with some of the same concepts; for in *G. Phil.* 65.1–26 the uniting of 'angels' and 'images' requested earlier in the eucharistic prayer is presented in greater detail as one of the core features of an apotropaic mechanism known as 'the bridal chamber', whose purpose as described in this second excerpt includes the protection of Christian initiates against sexually charged male and female spirits of impurity. To paraphrase the final few lines of the second excerpt: 'If the image [ⲉⲓⲕⲱⲛ] and the angel [ⲛⲁⲅⲅⲉⲗⲟⲥ] are united, no unclean male or female spirit can dare to make advances on the male or the female believer' (65.24–26).[50]

The brief eucharistic utterance attributed to Jesus in *G. Phil.* 58.11–14, therefore, is best understood as a performative ritual of request for a fresh instantiation of the bridal chamber and its apotropaic benefits as pictured in *G. Phil.* 65.1–26; and since the Jesus figure in *Philip* is emphatically paradigmatic for the Christian initiate,[51] that same request in 58.11–14 has strong potential to be taken up and used by initiates for purposes of reactivating the prophylaxis of the bridal chamber in eucharistic (and perhaps other) settings. But almost as importantly, by reading *G. Phil.* 58.10–14 and 65.1–26 together in the manner just proposed, we are now able to answer a difficult question raised by the latter of those two passages but not properly addressed by previous studies of it: namely, how does the Christian initiate gain access to or possession of the male power and the female power, the 'angel' and the 'image', essential for actualising the bridal chamber and its apotropaic benefits? The answer given indirectly by *G. Phil.* 58.10–14 is that the desired access or possession is facilitated by participation in a eucharistic ritual that includes the invocation attributed to Jesus in the cited prayer.[52]

In a sermon preached by John Chrysostom (c. 350–407) during his priesthood in Syrian Antioch,[53] the eucharist is explicitly represented as having a two-sided potential similar to that noted above in connection with John 13:26–30 and 1 Cor. 11:29. More specifically, in the course of expounding the controversy in John 6:42–52 over the eating of Jesus' flesh, Chrysostom emphasises that the love Christ has demonstrated by giving believers his own flesh to eat in the eucharist empowers them to arise 'from that table like lions exhaling fire, being fearsome to the devil'.[54] The visible presence of the eucharistic blood of Christ, Chrysostom adds, not only drives away demons and keeps them far away from believers but also attracts both a multitude of angels and 'the Lord of angels' himself,[55] an apotropaic scenario broadly similar to that inferred above from *G. Phil.* 58.10–14 and 65.1–26 but with a stronger group-orientation in Chrysostom. Yet the enjoyment of all this prophylaxis, Chrysostom reminds his audience, is conditioned upon the elements being approached 'with the utmost purity' (μετὰ καθαρότητος) and 'taken worthily';[56] indeed, to eat and drink unworthily of the Lord is in effect to eat and drink judgement against oneself, as Saint Paul warned the audience of his First Letter to the Corinthians (1 Cor. 11:29).[57] But perhaps most significantly for the present analysis, when Chrysostom concludes this same homily by warning his audience that 'those who receive the body [i.e., Christ's flesh in the eucharist] with impure intent suffer the same retribution as those who rent it with nails',[58] his implied prototype of punishable participation in the eucharist has come to consist largely of features identified above in the Johannine portrayal of Judas, whose blend of pervasive impurity (John 13:10–11), willingness to receive the bread/morsel whilst intending to do evil (John 13:2, 26–30), distinct vulnerability to diabolical influence (John 13:2, 27), and murderous enmity towards Jesus (John 18:3–5) resembles Chrysostom's negative prototype so closely it is surprising the latter includes no mention of Judas.

Finally, among the large number of amulets that have survived from various parts of the ancient world is a special subset whose strategies for accessing protective power include references to the Christian eucharist.[59] For instance, on a parchment amulet from fifth- or sixth-century Fayyum, the incipits of all four canonical Gospels in Greek are framed by a combination of brief excerpts from the biblical Psalter and the summary in Mt. 4:23 of Jesus' healings and other activities, directly followed by a liturgically stylised incantation that functions as a concluding petition: namely, 'The body and the blood of Christ spare your servant who carries this amulet. Amen, Hallelujah.'[60] The reference in that context not merely to Christ's blood but also to his body, in conjunction with the several liturgical features of the text as a whole, has prompted commentators to infer a eucharistic frame of reference for the final element.[61] Although the enemies implied by the spell are unspecified and thus include no explicit reference to demons, the vagueness in that connection is probably intended to enable the text to cover a wide range of threats, from hostile persons and general misfortune to various illnesses and the evil spirits assumed to cause them.[62]

Each of the comparative sources just discussed exemplifies a blend of assumptions and motifs which, taken as a whole, resembles the ideational mix inferred by the present reading of John 12–13. Indeed, the resemblances are sufficiently strong to warrant the suggestion that John 12:31 and 13:1–30 may have been read and heard in a similar fashion by enough early Christian audiences that they contributed in turn to the production of later texts such as those considered above. To test such a conjecture properly, a corpus of comparative materials wider than that treated above would need to be considered. That kind of inquiry cannot be conducted within the scope of the present study; but based on the comparative analysis initiated above, the parallels just discussed should not be allowed to overshadow what is almost certainly the most significant difference between the Johannine presentation and the other materials for purposes of the present chapter. Namely, neither the comparative texts just discussed nor any others of which I am aware conceptualise an exorcistic event as playing an essential role in the disciplinary exclusion of a group member at an association meal. Whatever challenges that conceptualisation may have posed to the clarity of John 12–13 as a piece of narrative discourse, its apparent creativity as an early Christian product of conceptual integration deserves more appreciation than it has hitherto received.

Notes

1 See J. S. Kloppenborg, *Christ's Associations: Connecting and Belonging in the Ancient City* (New Haven: Yale University Press, 2019); P. A. Harland, *Associations, Synagogues, and Congregations: Claiming a Place in Ancient Mediterranean Society* (Minneapolis: Fortress Press, 2003); D. E. Smith, *From Symposium to Eucharist: The Banquet in the Early Christian World* (Minneapolis: Fortress Press, 2003), 87–132; D. L. Balch and C. Osiek, *Families in the New Testament World: Households and House Churches* (Louisville: Westminster/John Knox, 1997), 193–214; L. T. Johnson, *Religious Experience in Earliest Christianity* (Minneapolis: Fortress Press, 1998), 137–79; and A. J. Malherbe, *Social Aspects of Early Christianity*, 2nd edn (Philadelphia: Fortress Press, 1983), 82–91, the last being a particularly helpful assessment of earlier treatments of the topic (e.g., G. Heinrici, E. Hatch, and E. A. Judge).
2 Harland, *Associations, Synagogues, and Congregations*, 2–3.
3 See Harland, *Associations, Synagogues, and Congregations*, 2, 14–18, 55–87.
4 See, e.g., D. Smith, *From Symposium to Eucharist*, 258, 264–65, 274; and Kobel, *Dining with John*, 275–93.
5 Comparative study of association banquet traditions was not a prominent feature of the academic context in which Thüsing's *Die Erhöhung und Verherrlichung Jesu im Johannesevangelium* was produced; and while the influence of such study has grown significantly in the last thirty years, it still has not been used to illuminate the theme of association discipline in John 13.
6 See John 6:67–71; 12:1–8; and 13:1–30.
7 I.e., the signalling of honest, difficult-to-fake, commitment to socioreligious cooperation. For summary and appraisal of recent theorising about religious ritual as signalling commitment to co-operation, see R. Uro, *Ritual and Christian Beginnings: A Socio-Cognitive Analysis* (Oxford: Oxford University Press, 2016), 133–48.
8 The ensuing analysis is largely an application of B. J. Malina's discussion of the more general phenomenon of honour challenge and riposte in ancient Mediterranean cultures of honour and shame; see Malina, *The New Testament World: Insights from Cultural Anthropology*, 3rd edn (Louisville: Westminster/John Knox, 2001), 38–43.
9 On the collective honour of a given social group being symbolised by the head of the group, see Malina, *The New Testament World*, 43–46.
10 The differences between the behaviours of Mary and Jesus in this context exemplify a 'gender division of labor' discussed by Malina, *The New Testament World*, 47, as characteristic of the ancient Mediterranean context.
11 P. R. Davies, G J. Brooke, and P. R. Calloway, *The Complete World of the Dead Sea Scrolls* (London: Thames & Hudson, 2002), 82.

12 The lexical collocation of ἐκβάλλω and ἐκκρίνω in the Josephan passage is a blending of the same word groups found together in John 12:31 (κρίσις ... ἐκβληθήσεται). Although the similarity between the two passages scarcely proves the case for a prophecy-fulfilment correspondence between John 12:31 and 13:30, it certainly increases the potential of John 12:31 to be read as showing interest not only in an exorcistic relocation of the satanic ruler but also in a paradigmatic expulsion of Judas as a dangerously uncooperative member of the group.
13 For purposes of comparative study of John 13:26–30, an especially striking feature in Philo's description of pagan meals is his adaptation of the Homeric story about the Cyclops and the companions of Odysseus (*Od.* 9.280–375 in *Contempl.* 40). In addition to suggesting that the pagan banquets are even more violent and disgraceful than the meal of human flesh that the Cyclops made of some of Odysseus's friends, Philo uses the noun ψωμίον to denote the bits of flesh consumed (and later, after much wine, vomited) by the monster. Thus, as in the setting of John 13:26–30 so also in *Contempl.* 40, the noun ψωμίον is used to denote human flesh as food in a meal involving conflict and hostile participants.
14 See, e.g., Harland, *Associations, Synagogues, and Congregations*, 74–75.
15 Cf. D. Smith, *From Symposium to Eucharist*, 119–25.
16 The possibility that the intratextual scenario described above in relation to Judas is analogous to the extratextual situation of 'the Johannine community' is entertained by Kobel, *Dining with John*, 288–92, chiefly in terms of the Christ association being betrayed to outsiders, but without comment on the motif of association discipline.
17 I.e., prior to Jesus' farewell speech (John 14–17) and thus before the banquet event has reached its end. The 'unexcused departure' by Judas is aptly described by Johnson, *Religious Experience*, 166, as a 'rupture of unity' and even as 'a kind of death'. The concept of expulsion/withdrawal from the group as a form of death has a parallel in 1 Cor. 5:1–13, where the recommended expulsion of the wrongdoer in that situation (5:13) is implicitly conceptualised as a causal factor in the anticipated destruction of his flesh (5:5); and a similar concept has recently been inferred by F. Watson, *What Is a Gospel?* (Grand Rapids: Wm. B. Eerdmans, 2022), 35–36, from John 13:30 to explain the absence of any account of Judas' death in the Fourth Gospel – from the evangelist's point of view, Judas dies symbolically as soon as he leaves the Jesus circle's final group supper.
18 I.e., what is both assumed and implied by the Johannine narrative is made grammatically explicit in Lk. 22:3–6, where the process of 'betrayal' signified by παραδῷ (v. 4) and παραδοῦναι (v. 6) is presented in clauses that not only have Judas as subject/actor and Jesus as object/goal but also include the dative indirect object αὐτοῖς – '... betray him *to them*', i.e., to the chief priests and the temple police – which gives the out-group authorities a defining role in the circumstances of the betrayal.
19 As indeed it is applied through the exorcistic drama narrated in John 13:1–30.
20 For the Greek text, see *IG* II.2 1368; for both the Greek text and an English translation, see R. A. Ascough, P. A. Harland, and J. S. Kloppenborg, 'Associations in the Greco-Roman World: An Expanding Collection of Inscriptions, Papyri, and Other Sources in Translation', accessed 23 January 2022, http://philipharland.com/greco-roman-associations/regulations-of-a-bacchic-association-the-iobacchoi/; and for analysis and further discussion, see D. Smith, *From Symposium to Eucharist*, 111–25.

21 In the given context the 'wand' (θύρσον) would have been a light, straight shaft wreathed in ivy and vine-leaves with a pinecone at its top. To the devotees of Bacchus, the wand was a numinous object that symbolised the presence and power of the god himself. See LSJ, s.v. 'θύρσον'.
22 Reading John 13:1–30 in terms of ancient association banquets and disciplinary codes has the additional strength of helping to explain the Johannine supper's lack of the full eucharist-institution formula present in the Pauline and Synoptic parallels (1 Cor. 11:23–25; Mt. 26:26–29; Mk 14:22–25; Lk. 22:15–20). The Fourth Gospel's strong interest in presenting the expulsion of Judas as an ethical paradigm for the Christ followers' community discipline in the evangelist's own situation is rightly judged by the Gospel's author as inconsistent in register, mood, and affectivity with the words of the institution, which has therefore been relocated to the story of Jesus' multiplication of loaves and fishes (John 6:53–54).
23 The attempt by R. A. Burridge, *Imitating Jesus: An Inclusive Approach to New Testament Ethics* (Grand Rapids: Wm B. Eerdmans, 2007), 339–46, e.g., to preserve the Fourth Gospel's imagined ethic of radical inclusivity, includes very little discussion of the Johannine Judas, and no discussion at all regarding how the portrayal of Judas in John 13:1–30 can be construed as cohering with the same radical ethic.
24 A recent articulation of the secessionist interpretation, with discussion of the scholarly origins and history of that view, is Martin, *Judas and the Rhetoric of Comparison*, 131–50.
25 Peter's suitability to the responsibilities of association bouncer – someone willing and able to use physical force to protect his friends – is consistent with his readiness to wield his sword against Malchus, the high priest's slave, in the setting of Jesus' arrest (John 18:10–11; par. Lk. 22:50); on association bouncers, see *IG* II.2 1368, lines 135–46.
26 On both the (in)equality of portion sizes and the importance of order and priority in service, see D. Smith, *From Symposium to Eucharist*, 116, 120, 124. Balch and Osiek, *Families in the New Testament World*, 195–96, highlight the reversal of normal hierarchies in Lucian's satire on the Saturnalia banquet, for which Chronos (as king of the feast) has legislated that all participants 'shall have their meat on equal terms ... . Neither are large portions to be placed before one and tiny ones before another, nor a ham for one and a pig's jaw for another – all must be treated equally (*Sat*. 17).
27 D. Smith, *From Symposium to Eucharist*, 116, 120.
28 See, e.g., Malherbe, *Social Aspects*, 82–83; Balch and Osiek, *Families in the New Testament World*, 198–204.
29 B. Kapferer, *A Celebration of Demons: Exorcism and the Aesthetic of Healing in Sri Lanka*, 2nd edn (Providence, R.I.: Berg; Washington, D.C.: Smithsonian Institution Press, 1991), 100–102.
30 A piece or scrap of food; see LSJ, s.v. 'ψωμίον'.
31 Neither Thyen, *Das Johannes-evangelium*, 600–603; Schnelle, *Das Evangelium nach Johannes*, 243; or Brown, *The Gospel according to John XIII–XXI*, 575, mentions the diminutive character of the form. Barrett, *The Gospel according to St John*, 447–48, notes it briefly but does not comment on either the difference in meaning between ψωμός and ψωμίον or its potential significance in the given context.
32 For a concise summary of these two 'movements' in the larger process of translation, see G. Steiner, *After Babel: Aspects of Language and Translation*, 3rd edn (Oxford: Oxford University Press, 1998), 313–16.

33 See John 2:1–11 (esp. vv. 5–7); 4:7–15 (esp. vv. 13–15); 6:1–59 (esp. vv. 11–13, 26–27, 35, 48–51); and 21:1–14 (esp. vv. 6, 8, and 11); all of which is perceptively taken by D. Smith, *From Symposium to Eucharist*, 273, as a literary-theological emphasis on the numinous quality of the food provided by the Johannine Jesus, but without considering the implications of that theme for understanding the morsel in John 13:26–30.

34 On the theme of in-group love, note especially the progression from 'you ... ought to wash one another's feet' (John 13:14); to 'you ... should love one another' (13:34); and finally, to 'No one has greater love than this, to lay down one's life for one's friends' (15:13).

35 In regard to the expulsion of group members as a recognised practice of association ethics and discipline in the ancient social world of the author and intended audience of the Fourth Gospel, the Gospel's three references to the possibility of the Johannine Jesus' followers being expunged from Judaean assemblies (John 9:22; 12:42; and 16:2) confirm the ancient author's familiarity with ideas like those attributed to him in the present chapter and suggest a historically plausible context of prior experience from which he may have acquired his knowledge (i.e., ancient Judaean assemblies). The passages just referenced from John's Gospel are treated together in Kloppenborg, *Christ's Associations*, 341, as parallel to the disciplinary expulsion implied by Paul in 1 Cor. 5:5, noted for similar purposes above; but Kloppenborg's study joins many others in overlooking the evidence for association-style discipline in the Johannine episode of Judas' departure from the Jesus circle (John 13:26–30).

36 My suggestion here arises from a reading of H. Taussig, *In the Beginning Was the Meal: Social Experimentation and Early Christian Identity* (Minneapolis: Fortress, 2009), 66; cited in R. Uro, 'Ritual and the Rise of the Early Christian Movement', in *The Early Christian World*, 2nd edn, ed. P. F. Esler (London: Routledge, 2017), 435.

37 My inference here that Judas, as the exception, knows Jesus is talking about him at this point (v. 10) is derived from the narrator's comment in 13:2 that the devil had put the betrayal plot into Judas' heart by the beginning of the meal. By contrast, the uncertainty of Peter and John at minimum, but probably also the other disciples (except for Judas), is presented as continuing at least until the giving of the morsel in v. 27.

38 Regarding both the discursive ambiguity and the integration of ritual-symbolic action in this section, a path of inquiry that cannot be explored fully here but could lead to worthwhile insights in future research is whether both of those sets of phenomena should be seen as partly motivated by considerations of politeness. More precisely, since Jesus' goal of removing Judas from the group is inherently impolite – it is, after all, partly a riposte to the insulting behaviour attributed to Judas in John 12:4–5 – the combination of indirectness and ambiguity in Jesus' utterances and symbolic actions should perhaps be considered an instance of what G. Leech calls 'negative politeness', i.e., an attempt to minimise the impoliteness of intrinsically impolite speech or actions. Thus, although the communicative behaviour of Jesus in John 13:1–30 is not maximally direct or perspicuous on a scale of clarity, its obliqueness serves to minimise the impoliteness of his message and goal, which are clear enough for Judas in particular to get the point (13:30); the same behaviour also succeeds in upholding 'the maxim of relation' (i.e., 'the relevance principle') since it contributes to the goals of Jesus in the given speech situation. Indeed, the achievement of Jesus' social goal in this context – the exclusion of Judas from the group, preferably without need for physically coercive eviction – should perhaps be viewed as partly a result of Jesus' 'negative politeness'; and thus,

amongst the many qualities attributed to Jesus in John 13:1–30, one that deserves far more attention than it has been given in scholarly interpretation is his high level of social and communicative skill. The importance of politeness in maintaining 'face', both of self and of others, is recognised not only in linguistics but also in social anthropology. See, e.g., Carrithers, *Why Humans Have Cultures*, 60–63; and G. Leech, *The Principles of Pragmatics* (London and New York: Longman, 1983), 79–103.

39 Kapferer, *A Celebration of Demons*, 246–48.
40 A. van Gennep, *Rites of Passage*, trans. M. B. Vizedom and G. L. Caffee (Chicago: University of Chicago Press, 1961); V. W. Turner, *The Forest of Symbols: Aspects of Ndembu Ritual* (Ithaca: Cornell University Press, 1967); id., *The Ritual Process: Structure and Anti-Structure* (Harmondsworth: Penguin, 1969); and id., *Dramas, Fields, and Metaphors: Symbolic Action in Human Society* (Ithaca: Cornell University Press, 1974).
41 Discussed above on pp. 78–79.
42 On conceptual blending as a general cognitive capacity operative in everyday human thought and language, see the ground-breaking book by G. Fauconnier and M. Turner, *The Way We Think: Conceptual Blending and the Mind's Hidden Complexities* (New York: Basic Books, 2002). As Fauconnier and Turner (pp. 37–38) explain, the core operation is the creative integration of existing elements of meaning from different domains. The evidence for such an operation in John 13:26–30 is that the ideational content of this passage is at least partly the result of exorcism and eucharist being imaginatively brought together into a single integrated conceptual space where previously, as far as our sources allow us to see, the two concepts existed only separately.
43 See especially C. E. Hill, *The Johannine Corpus in the Early Church* (Oxford: Oxford University Press, 2004), 421–43, whose argument specifically for Ignatian knowledge of the Fourth Gospel is impressively well-informed and weighs strongly against the dominant critical alternative ('orthodox Johannophobia'), but whose presentation as a whole has been rightly criticised by K. Keefer, Review of *The Johannine Corpus in the Early Church* , by Charles E. Hill, *JBL* 124 (2005): 189, for a tendency to exaggerate the power of its own analysis; a tendency exemplified by the first sentence of the conclusion to Hill's treatment of the Ignatius question: 'Ignatius' knowledge of John can be taken as proved' (p. 442).
44 Twelftree, *In the Name of Jesus*, 228–29.
45 Twelftree does not include an explicit definition of the concept of exorcism used in his book, *In the Name of Jesus*; but a hard-edged, sea-shell category of the sort criticised by Carrithers, *Why Humans Have Cultures*, 12–33, is apparent in Twelftree's comment that Tobias's success in driving away Asmodeus may not have been considered by the author of Tobit to be 'an exorcism' (p. 37). In response we might query, first, whether the Book of Tobit affords evidence for thinking its author even had a clearly defined concept of exorcism such as Twelftree's; but also why, even if the ancient author did have such a concept, it ought to be accorded prescriptive force in the construction of a category whose main purpose is to facilitate comparative analysis of Tobit and other ancient sources some of which the author of Tobit could not have known (e.g., the Synoptic Gospels). With consequences more directly relevant to the present part of my analysis, the same problematic construction of 'exorcism' as a category weakens Twelftree's treatment of 'exorcism' and its 'absence' in the Fourth Gospel (pp. 183–204) and Ignatius of Antioch (pp. 226–29); more particularly, and perhaps because his tightly bounded construction of the category militates against either John 13:26–30 or Ign., *Eph.* 13.1

being construed as broadly exorcistic, he has nothing to say about either the analogical or the genealogical potential of the comparison.

46 Σπουδάζετε οὖν πυκνότερον συνέρχεσθαι εἰς εὐχαριστίαν θεοῦ καὶ εἰς δόξαν, with εὐχαριστίαν θεοῦ having potential to signify a simple giving of thanks to God; but more probably having the sense of 'God's eucharist' in this context, especially considering Ignatius's development of similar themes later in the same letter, where the congregating of Ephesian Christ-followers is closely associated with their breaking of 'one bread' as the 'medicine of immortality' (20.2). For the non-eucharistic rendering, see B. D. Ehrman (ed.), *The Apostolic Fathers*, vol. 1, LCL 24 (Cambridge, MA: Harvard University Press, 2003), 233; and J. B. Lightfoot and J. R. Harmer, *The Apostolic Fathers: Revised Greek Texts with Introductions and English Translations* (London: Macmillan and Co., 1891), 140. For the eucharistic interpretation, see the parenthetical suggestion in Ehrman (id.); BAGD, s.v. 'εὐχαριστία'; and W. R. Schoedel, *Ignatius of Antioch: A Commentary on the Letters of Ignatius of Antioch*, Hermeneia (Philadelphia: Fortress, 1985), 74.

47 H. Lundhaug, *Images of Rebirth: Cognitive Poetics and Transformational Soteriology in the Gospel of Philip and the Exegesis on the Soul*, NHMS 73 (Leiden: Brill, 2010), 6–13.

48 The English translation of the narrator's introductory clause, above, is Lundhaug's (*Images of Rebirth*, 280, 284), which has the merit of making explicit the eucharistic-ritual context inferred by most other commentators; see, e.g., M. L. Turner, *The Gospel according to Philip: The Sources and Coherence of an Early Christian Collection*, NHMS 38 (Leiden: Brill, 1996), 178–79. The reason a eucharistic ritual should be understood here, as opposed to a more general prayer of thanksgiving, consists partly of the eucharistic interests indicated elsewhere in *Philip* (e.g., 63.21–24; 74.24–36; 75.14–24; 77.2–6) and partly of the prayer's greater stylistic proximity to an epiclesis (i.e., a eucharistic invitation of the Holy Spirit to bless the elements or the communicants) than to a more general utterance of thanksgiving.

49 Lundhaug, *Images of Rebirth*, 279–81.

50 The paraphrase above is based on the discourse-analytic interpretation in T. E. Klutz, 'Inside the Bridal Chamber: Individual, Group and Intertextuality in *Gospel of Philip* 65.1–26', in *Scripture as Social Discourse: Social-Scientific Perspectives on Early Jewish and Christian Writings*, ed. J. M. Keady, T. E. Klutz, and C. A. Strine (ed.), (London: T & T Clark 2018), 211–232.

51 See, e.g., K. L. King, 'The Place of the *Gospel of Philip* in the Context of Early Christian Claims about Jesus' Marital Status', *NTS* 59.4 (2013): 572–86.

52 The close relationship entailed by the interpretation above, between the eucharistic and bridal chamber concepts in *Philip*, is recognised by Lundhaug, *Images of Rebirth*, 330, despite his exegesis of *G. Phil.* 58.10–14 as having no meaningful connection to 65.1–26. Despite showing no interest in John 13:21–30, Lundhaug rightly highlights strong affinities between *Philip* and the Fourth Gospel regarding the eucharist (p. 284).

53 For recent discussion situating Chrysostom in the cultural context of early eastern Christianity, see W. Mayer and P. Allen, 'John Chrysostom', *The Early Christian World*, 1054–71.

54 *In Joannem* 59.260.53–61 (trans. mine).

55 *In Joannem* 59.261.18–22.

56 *In Joannem* 59.262.28; and 59.261.18.

57 *In Joannem* 59.262.29–32.

58 *In Joannem* 59.262.32–36 (trans. mine).

59 See, e.g., E. Chepel, 'Invocations of the Blood of Christ in Greek Magical Amulets', *Scrinium* 13 (2017): 58–59, 62–66.
60 For the Greek text and discussion, see Chepel, 'Invocations', 58, 62–64; for an English translation including crosses and other visual symbols, see M. Meyer and R. Smith (ed), *Ancient Christian Magic: Coptic Texts of Ritual Power* (San Francisco: HarperCollins, 1994), 34–35.
61 E.g., Chepel, 'Invocations', 63–65.
62 Chepel, 'Invocations', 62–64. A similar instance of functional vagueness is inferred by R. Mazza from the opening line of a sixth- or seventh-century Christian prayer amulet constituting one side of P. Ryl. Greek Add. 1166, whose reference to the eucharistic body and blood of Christ (lines 10–11) – the 'manna of the new covenant' (lines 8–9; cf. John 6:25–59) – is implied to be a cause of fear to 'all who rule over the earth' (i.e., all categories of evil, according to Mazza, including malevolent spirits); R. Mazza, 'P. Ryl. Greek Add. 1166: Christian Prayer Amulet with a Tax Receipt on the Back', *ZPE* 197 (2016): 76–83.

5 Conclusion

Summary of Findings

The preceding chapters begin by assessing the two most widely accepted scholarly suggestions regarding what sort of event narrated in the Fourth Gospel is best understood as fulfilling the Johannine Jesus' prophecy about the expulsion of 'the ruler of this world' (John 12:31). Serious shortcomings in the prevailing views are identified by analysing their treatment of the key passage and its narrative co-text from a perspective informed by Critical Discourse Analysis and the cognitive-linguistic distinction between 'container metaphors' and 'orientational metaphors'. That same perspective informs a re-reading of John 12:31 that identifies widely overlooked collocational and other types of chains between the immediate co-text of that passage and material surrounding the subsequent narration of Judas departure from the Jesus circle in John 13:30. Reinforced as those chains are by the presence of container metaphors in both passages, the analysis gathers evidence in support of a widely overlooked proposal made by Wilhelm Thüsing in the second edition of a monograph originally published in 1960: namely, instead of understanding the predicted expulsion of the ruler as corresponding to his being either thrown down from heaven or cast out of the cosmos altogether, we should interpret the expulsion as consisting of a sequence of broadly exorcistic actions by Jesus that culminate in the satanically possessed Judas being relocated outside the metaphorical container/circle consisting of Jesus and the other disciples in John 13:21–31.

This suggestion has several noteworthy implications for the interpretation of John's Gospel. For instance, it entails that the relationship between Jesus' utterance in John 12:31b and Judas' withdrawal from the group in 13:30 has the character of a prophecy-fulfilment scheme, which in its turn enhances both the textual cohesion and the metaphorical coherence of John 12–13 and the Gospel as a whole. In terms of theological themes and Christological rhetoric, moreover, the same proposal coheres with and contributes to the Fourth Gospel's foregrounded

DOI: 10.4324/9781003359319-5

Conclusion 85

interest in the truthfulness and reliability of the word of Jesus as a legitimate prophet. And, indirectly, it also reopens for discussion the difference between the Fourth Gospel and the Synoptics regarding exorcism; for although neither Judas nor any other individual character in the Fourth Gospel is portrayed as being healed through the expulsion of a demon, Judas' vulnerability to diabolical influence from his first appearing in the Fourth Gospel (6:70–71) worsens across the narrative until he finally becomes possessed by Satan (13:27), with the result that his withdrawal from the Jesus circle in John 13:30–31 is simultaneously a relocating of the satanic ruler now inside him; thus, while Satan is never portrayed in John as being driven out of Judas, both the Johannine Satan and Judas are expelled from the Jesus circle through a process that resembles a range of other exorcistic events attested in ancient Mediterranean sources.

According to this same proposal, although a broadly exorcistic register of discourse is introduced in John 12:31 by Jesus' use of ἐκβάλλω in conjunction with the satanological phrase ὁ ἄρχων τοῦ κόσμου τούτου, the verb in that context projects the exorcistic expulsion as taking place in the future; but in the ensuing co-text nothing resembling an exorcism is narrated until John 13:26–30. In that context, the rapid succession of Jesus giving Judas the morsel, Satan immediately entering into Judas, Jesus issuing a broadly incantatory command to the possessed Judas, and Judas going out from the group suggests that scholarly discourse about 'the absence of exorcism in the Fourth Gospel' has not been as thoughtful as it should have been in its construction of 'exorcism' for purposes of comparative analysis of John, the Synoptics, and other relevant materials from antiquity on this point. In contrast, by taking seriously the potential for exorcistic overtones in John 12:31 and 13:26–30, the present interpretation enables the reader to recognise the similarities between the exiting of the possessed Judas in John 13:30 and the withdrawal of exorcised demons in the Synoptic Gospels and Acts on the one hand, and between the Johannine Jesus' exorcistic strategy in John 13:26–30 and the exorcistic techniques attested in the Synoptics and various other ancient sources on the other hand.

By the time Jesus pronounces his prophecy in John 12:31 about the expulsion of the ruler, Judas has been characterised repeatedly in the bleakest of terms. The very devil himself (6:70), the future betrayer of Jesus (6:71), an unbeliever who deceptively stays amongst the circle of believing disciples (6:60–71), who takes offence at Jesus teaching about his own body and blood (6:52–65), who criticises others for their costly gestures of commitment to Jesus' and misrepresents himself as caring for the poor (12:4–6) – all of this blame has been attached to Judas in the Fourth Gospel before the text's audience hears the prediction about the ruler in John 12:31. Not surprisingly, therefore, after the key utterance in 12:31 but prior to the narration of the possessed Judas' departure from

86 *Conclusion*

the group in 13:30, yet another negative quality is attributed to the betrayer: namely, that of a pervasive impurity, an uncleanness that cannot be removed by footwashing (13:10–11) or even by reception of the eucharistic morsel (13:26–30); and since the diabolical character of Judas' identity is almost certainly understood by the Gospel's implied author to preclude the possibility of his exercising faith in Jesus (as the only way to undergo the thorough bathing he needs, 13:10), Judas himself and the diabolical ruler he eventually contains must be expunged from the Jesus circle (13:26–30).

As in the Synoptic accounts of exorcism, therefore, so also in the exorcistic relocation of the Johannine Judas, the expulsion of the diabolical power is simultaneously an act of purification, though in the Johannine context an attendant process of religious innovation can be inferred whereby the relevant concepts of clean and unclean have been redefined so as to have less to do with Second Temple Jewish codes of impurity than with loyalty to the Jesus figure portrayed in the Fourth Gospel. In addition, while the beneficiary of the exorcistic purification in the Synoptics is primarily the individual patient and only secondarily the patient's social network, in John 13 the role of beneficiary is filled very largely or even entirely by the immediate in-group of believing disciples, for whom the departure of Judas entails the removal of a dangerous form of pollution.

The significance of the dinner scene from which Judas withdraws in John 13:30 is constrained and enriched by the meal episodes presented earlier in the Gospel. Both John 6:1–71 and 12:1–8 anticipate several of the complicating actions and key themes encountered in the supper, footwashing, and exorcism sequence in John 13:1–30. Since Judas is implicitly identified in John 6:64–71 not only as an unbeliever but also as distinctly diabolical, the sharp command addressed to him later by Jesus in response to Judas' attempt to shame Mary over her use of the costly perfume – 'Get away from her!' (12:7) – has a broadly apotropaic quality that anticipates the more dramatic intervention in John 13:21–30. But since both the sequencing of the actions in the latter section and the logical relations implied by the syntax of verses 26–27 and 30 have the effect of presenting the morsel, given by Jesus to Judas at the end of the scene, as instrumental in the exorcistic process of relocating Judas, those parts of the scene recall both the portrayal of Jesus in John 6 as someone capable of performing supramundane deeds with ordinary things such as bread and fishes, and the potential of those same deeds to be perceived in ways that occasion offence.

As early as John 6:60–65, and thus before Judas has even been mentioned by name, he is implicitly identified as one of those who take offence at the idea of Jesus' flesh and blood as food and drink; and since from that point onward he is compared negatively with other characters

Conclusion 87

in the narrative and is consistently portrayed as lacking faith in Jesus, his action of receiving the morsel from Jesus lends itself to interpretation in later contexts of reading/hearing as an example of unworthy reception of the eucharist (i.e., partaking of it without discerning the body of Jesus). In the context of early Christian celebrations of the Lord's Supper, the danger posed by that sort of partaking had been addressed decades earlier by Paul in 1 Cor. 11. Although the rhetorical situation of 1 Cor. 11:17–34 is scarcely the same as that of John 13:21–30, Paul's teaching about eating and drinking in a manner worthy of the Lord has potential to illuminate both what happens to Judas in the Johannine passage – especially vv. 26–27 and 30 – and why it happens. In brief, Judas' reception of the morsel not only directly precedes his becoming completely possessed by Satan, but also helps to bring it about; and the reason it does so is that it involves partaking of the Lord's flesh without the requisite faith and attitude.

Yet the tightening of Satan's grip on Judas is not the only harmful consequence of Judas' faithless reception of the food from Jesus; for the food-possession connection in 13:27 – 'After the morsel, Satan entered into him' – is firmly chain-linked to the presentation of Judas' departure from the group: 'Therefore, having received the morsel, he immediately went out' (13:30). From the hands of John's incarnate logos, therefore, a little morsel of the eucharist is able not only to lure Satan into Judas but also to drive both Judas and the diabolical ruler he now embodies out and away from the fledgling community of the faithful. Thus, in addition to serving a purificatory purpose for the association of believing disciples, the exorcistic event that completes the prophecy-fulfilment scheme inferred from John 12:31 and 13:30 also sets forth a ritual paradigm for handling the presence of in-group unbelievers in the context of the Gospel's reception: namely, in their meetings for instruction and fellowship, the Christ cult should avail themselves of the ritual power of Christ's body and blood in the eucharist to provide protection against the devil and to drive away his agents of unbelief, falsehood, and treachery.

Although the conceptual blending of broadly exorcistic activities and processes of ritual purification are attested in various contexts (including that of the Synoptic Gospels) prior to the composition of the Gospel according to John, the hints of an exorcistic function for the eucharist in John 13 have no clear precursor in Christ-group sources likely to have been available to the author of the Fourth Gospel. In that light, it is possible that the integration of eucharist and exorcism inferred above is an instance of religious innovation on the part of the Gospel's author, though other explanations for the origin of this idea should not be ruled out. But just as importantly, whatever the origins of this blend might be, the conceptual integration of eucharist and exorcism has been demonstrated above to have circulated widely from early in the second century

CE to the fifth or sixth centuries, in forms ranging from letters highlighting the benefits of eucharistic meetings, to apotropaic amulets that include appeals to the eucharist alongside citations of biblical texts, eucharistic prayers in Valentinian texts seeking ritual re-enactments of the bridal chamber and its apotropaic benefits, and rhetorically eloquent homilies that interpret the Johannine narration of Jesus' feeding miracle and discourse about the 'bread of life' (John 6) as illustrating the cosmic power of the eucharist to make demons flee from the faithful.

Many or even most of the meanings summarised above, however, would never see the light of day were we insistent on approaching the key passages in John 12–13 with the same narrow, tidy, clear-edged definition of 'exorcism' that is normally assumed in scholarly discourse about 'the absence of exorcism' in the Fourth Gospel. By expanding our concept of 'exorcism' to create space for recognising a range of ritual events which, while not exorcisms in a constricted sense, exemplify notable degrees of family resemblance to an exorcism prototype, the present study has been able to read John 12:31 in a way that avoids the difficulties of the normal readings and enables several passages in the Fourth Gospel to become more coherent and meaningful pieces of narrative discourse. Two additional ways in which those results have been achieved are worthy of restatement as the final points of the present summary.

By construing the narration of Judas' departure from the meal in John 13:30 as completing a prophecy-fulfilment scheme initiated by Jesus' prior utterance about the satanic ruler (12:31), the present study has been able to infer several significant similarities between the meal scene in John 13 and historical models of association banquets studied in recent decades by scholars of religion in Mediterranean antiquity. Although the same analogy has been suggested in general terms by others, it has not been explored in those studies at the level of particular motifs and grammatical detail. The space afforded by the present inquiry for constructing illuminating analogies has allowed the following point of special interest to be developed in the preceding chapters.

The characterisation of Judas in John 6:60–71 and 12:1–8 is interpreted in the present study as possessing a frequently overlooked layer of social meaning when it is viewed in the light of disciplinary codes for behaviour at association banquets in the wider social context of early Christianity. By the standards of suitable behaviour at ancient banqueting events, after the insults Judas hurls at all the named participants in the meal narrated in John 12:1–8, he should be understood as having dishonoured the Jesus circle and its head in ways that would warrant at least temporary exclusion if not permanent dismissal from the group. Additionally, since Jesus is the main target of Judas' negative challenge in John 12:6, Jesus' brief riposte in defence of Mary alone in John 12:7–8 leaves ample scope for a more robust counter-challenge to Judas later in the narrative. Much of the anticipated counter-blast by Jesus comes in the prophecy-fulfilment scheme in John 12:31b and 13:1–30, with Jesus aiming a barrage of innuendos (e.g., 'Not all of you are clean', 13:11) and symbolic actions against Judas' status until Judas finally leaves the group and takes Satan with him. The exorcistic process that fulfils the prophetic utterance in John 12:31b, therefore, also serves to satisfy the kinds of disciplinary codes and in-group rules for excluding offensive banqueters at meetings of ancient associations as diverse as the Qumran community, the Therapeutae, the Athenian Iobacchoi, and the Christ-following congregation in St Paul's Corinth.

Narratives and other genres of discourse about exorcism often exemplify interest in both the ultimate destination of successfully expelled spirits and their movement through space en route to such places. Expunged demons can be trapped inside a leather flask, transferred to the environs of a hostile nation, required to shake a nearby statue, imprisoned in the body of an unclean animal, allowed to wander for a time through waterless places (before returning to their former host), or simply banned from ever returning. In that light, the analysis above has considered where the satanic ruler in the Fourth Gospel is described as going once his container 'goes out' (13:30) from the Jesus circle.

The well-known aside by the Gospel's narrator in 13:30 – 'And it was night' – has the overt function of orientating the Gospel's audience to Judas' departure not in terms of space but rather in time and thus on the surface may seem to give away nothing about where Judas may be headed. Yet the combination of the widely recognised potential for symbolic meaning in that reference, and the use of closely related indicators of time later in the narrative,[1] suggests that the reference here to time has metaphorically extended potential to convey extra meaning, some of it having to do with space. Significantly, although Judas is mentioned three times by the Johannine Jesus between Judas' withdrawal from the group and his re-entry into the main storyline of the Gospel, the point at which he re-enters the plot of main narrated actions is placed by the narrator in an outdoor garden-setting of darkness, where the soldiers and police need lanterns for vision in their search for Jesus, and where the glimmers of dawn are still too faint for the cock to have crowed in fulfilment of the prediction Jesus gave Peter shortly after Judas' departure (13:38). From the narrator's point of view, all of that is very dark indeed, in more ways than one. But from a more strictly spatial point of view, in that same dark setting of Judas' re-entry, his anticipated return with the satanic 'ruler of this world' is both foregrounded and given new meaning by his new position in public space: namely, as the guide for a combination of armed Roman forces and Judaean police that have come for Jesus' arrest, with Judas positioning himself 'with them' – and thus against Jesus – once the proceedings of the arrest are underway.

90 Conclusion

With Judas having been closely associated with the devil from his first appearance in the larger Gospel narrative onwards, the characterisation of both the Roman maniple and the Judean police as willing to be guided by him (John 18:2–4) implies that those parties have no more respect for Jesus and his followers than Judas does. Similarly, in their reaction to Jesus' 'I am' utterance in the same setting (18:5), the combination of soldiers, police, and Judas all withdraw backwards as a single undifferentiated unit. It is scarcely insignificant, politically or in any other respect, who the satanic ruler in this context is presented as aligning himself with in the aftermath of his prophecy-fulfilling expulsion by Jesus in John 13:26–30. Nonetheless, Judas remains for the implied author of the Fourth Gospel both the metaphorical container and the primary agent of the satanic ruler; and far from having been somehow cast out of the cosmos, in their final appearance on the stage of the Fourth Gospel both Judas and the satanic ruler are more manifestly confined to the world than at any previous point in John's story of Jesus.

Concluding Reflection and Implications for Further Research

In the summary above and at several points in the preceding chapters, the potential for mutually illuminating dialogue between the present study and scholarship on the Fourth Gospel's lack of Synoptic-style exorcism accounts has been mentioned. The latter of those topics, however, has been given only brief attention in the present inquiry, partly to ensure that the discussion be kept within suitable limits, but also because the idea of 'Synoptic-style exorcism accounts' has been instrumental in the scholarly construction of 'exorcism' as a category too narrow for purposes of interpreting John 12–13.

But now that the present study has nearly reached its end, and with the path to that end having been mapped with the aid of a consciously broadened definition of 'exorcism', an agenda for one area of potentially fruitful research in the future can be sketched by asking whether the preceding pages have any noteworthy implications for that separate but closely related question about the absence of exorcism (now, clearly, only in the narrow sense) in the Gospel of John. A possibility I intend to develop fully in a separate monograph, and which I hereby invite others to consider with me, is that the phenomenon of individual unbelief identified above as constituting the core of Judas' 'uncleanness' (John 13:10–11) could easily have been understood by the author of John's Gospel as very similar to a characteristic attributed to most or all of the demoniacs healed by Jesus in the exorcism stories and related traditions of the Synoptic Gospels. To be precise, none of the individual demoniacs depicted in the Synoptic accounts is ever presented as exemplifying faith in Jesus prior to the climax of exorcistic release that Jesus achieves for

Conclusion 91

them. In two exorcism accounts included in the Synoptics, Jesus intervenes partly because a parent of the demoniac initially shows some measure of faith in Jesus as healer;[2] but that type of scenario only serves to underscore what could easily have struck the author of the Fourth Gospel as a significant problem in his Synoptic sources. Namely, the most direct beneficiary of the exorcistic healing, the patient themselves, neither demonstrates faith towards Jesus nor, very probably, would they have been able to do so since the logic of demon possession entails a loss of individual agency on the part of the possessed.

The likelihood that the author of the Fourth Gospel would have read the Synoptic materials about demoniacs and exorcism in the manner just suggested is strengthened by certain clear features in the Johannine depiction of Judas. For instance, although Jesus is characterised in John as having been accused by his Judean opponents of 'having a demon', the only character presented by the narrator of the Fourth Gospel as having actually become indwelt by an evil spirit is Judas; and once the Johannine Judas becomes a spirit-possessed container for Satan (John 13:27), he not only continues to walk along his dark path of unbelief but follows it all the way to taking his stand with Jesus' enemies in the setting of the arrest. But just as importantly, since the chapters above have seen a blending of both realist and symbolic features in the Johannine characterisation of Judas, the antithesis of diabolical possession and salvific faith in that portrayal has considerable symbolic potential to point beyond itself to a more general conviction in the ideological orientation of the Fourth Gospel. Namely, the type of faith promoted by the author of that Gospel is not appropriately modelled by the demoniacs portrayed in the Synoptic tradition.

Accordingly, from the standpoint of the author of the Fourth Gospel, the exorcism accounts in his Synoptic sources simply had to go. But if, as just suggested, the reason Synoptic exorcisms had to be omitted in the Fourth Gospel is that they implicitly conflicted with John's emphasis on the soteriological necessity of faith on the part of each individual member of the Christ-group – something that demoniacs lacked the agency to do – the question may rightly be asked why John wished to reframe faith and elevate its importance in such a manner. Although that question cannot be taken up satisfactorily here, any exploration of it in future research may wish to consider an explanation close enough to the present discussion to warrant brief mention at its close. As scholarship on the Fourth Gospel becomes increasingly confident that the author of that writing was acquainted not only with the Gospel of Mark but also with Luke and perhaps also Matthew, it may also become increasingly open to the theory that John's distinctively emphatic representation of faith as a condition for eternal life and membership in the messianic community was initially formulated as a revision of certain Synoptic, but perhaps also partly Pauline, images of salvation and the community of the saved; comparatively inclusive conceptions, moreover, which not only contributed to the rapid growth of Christ assemblies in their first several decades but also courted the risk of attracting free-riders, uncooperative members, and persons whom the author of John 15:1–8 might have conceptualised as fruitless vines that ought to be cast out.

In a rhetorical situation shaped along those lines, the Johannine narration of the expulsion of Judas would have communicated with a very high degree of contextual relevance; and the coherence of that same story with its larger narrative co-text would only have been strengthened by the same author's bold move of omitting traditions he undoubtedly knew which portrayed Jesus as a healer of demoniacs, of persons lacking the agency, that is, requisite to exercising the individual faith essential for experiencing the healed life of the messianic age in Jesus.

In the situation imagined above, therefore, is to be recognised a vague but discernible sense of individualism, not of course in the modern western form by which we know it today but rather in the lived assumption that, in their respective contexts of collective embedding and group-oriented identity, ancient Mediterranean persons possessed individual agency, inevitably experienced what can suitably be called 'individuation', and made individual decisions which contributed to the meaning of their own daily lives and that of their families, neighbours, and communities. Individualism, in something like the sense just defined, has been discussed previously in scholarship on the Fourth Gospel, with notable contributions from C. F. D. Moule and, more recently, Richard Bauckham.[3] However, as in the field of Gnostic and Nag Hammadi studies so also in Johannine scholarship, a full and systematic study of individualism and the various ways in which it inevitably presupposes and is blended with collectivist outlooks and practices is yet to be published.[4] If such a project is ever undertaken, it cannot hope to be adequate if it fails to consider the combined effect of the Johannine portrayal of Judas and the absence of the exorcism stories in the larger framework of the same Gospel.

But finally, the present study would be remiss if it failed to highlight that the interplay between the Johannine Judas as a representative of individual unbelief and the Jesus circle, as an association whose collective purity is protected by Judas' expulsion, has potentially profound relevance to a wide range of discourses outside the field of biblical studies. In an impressive series of books and essays on the broader subject of religion in Roman antiquity, the classical philologist Jörg Rüpke has mounted a serious challenge to the widespread scholarly image of Roman religion as a rigid system of ritual allowing little or no room for individual variance, arguing on the contrary that the interplay of reading and ritual performance attested for a wide range of settings

Conclusion 93

around the early imperial period give evidence of 'a process of long-term, reflective religious individualization'.[5] In an equally remarkable work offering a much longer, genealogical and developmental view of individualism, the cultural historian Larry Siedentop has suggested that John's Gospel and its early reception contributed to an understanding of God as the 'foundation of individual being', individual faith in Christ, and thus the individual 'potential for freedom' essential to the eventual emergence of western liberalism.[6] And from the different but largely complementary perspectives of a professional philosopher and a team of modern sociologists of religion in America, Charles Taylor and a group of social-scientists led by Robert Bellah have produced penetrating analyses of American and other, largely modern western varieties of individualism, arguing that the corrosive effects of extreme individualism on solidarity and social cohesion in modern society are difficult to disentangle from Christianity's long contribution to individualistic modes of being religious and thinking about religion.[7]

Academics in diverse disciplines and reflective thinkers in non-academic fields of endeavour have been exercising their minds for many decades on the human problem of being an intrinsically social type of animal that possesses at the same time a drive – in many instances, a very powerful drive – to individuation. Although the Gospel of John was produced in a cultural context known to be more strongly group-oriented, and thus less individualising, than that in which the author and readers of the present book are likely to have been socialised, it exemplifies a remarkably innovative reimagining not only of Judas the betrayer and his departure from the Jesus circle but also of the role played by the individual Christ-follower in the safety and productivity of the larger association of believers. Indeed, since the Gospel of John continues to be widely read, quoted, and preached in the United States, as well as in other contexts where 'the hegemonic character of present day individualism' reminds us daily that we must be individuals[8] – unrelenting seekers, that is, of what Taylor calls 'expressive individualism' – that same ancient gospel text may have potential to inspire much-needed critique of our current modes of blending individualist and collectivist values, and thereby to assist us in fashioning wiser and healthier ways of being human.

Notes

1 Consider, e.g., the sequence of John 13:38 ('before the cock crows'); 18:3 ('lanterns and torches'); and 18:27 ('the cock crowed').
2 See Mt. 15:21–28; par. Mk 7:24–30; and Mt. 17:14–21; par. Mk 9:14–29 and Lk. 9:37–43a.
3 See C. F. D. Moule, 'The Individualism of the Fourth Gospel', *NovT* 5 (1962): 171–90; and R. J. Bauckham, *Gospel of Glory: Major Themes in Johannine Theology* (Grand Rapids: Baker Academic, 2015), 1–19.

4 As proposed below, a comprehensive study would give attention not only to what is highlighted in John but also to what John omits. A recent approach along those lines has been applied to select Nag Hammadi tractates in Klutz, 'Inside the Bridal Chamber', in *Scripture as Social Discourse*, 211–32; and Klutz, 'From Temple to Desert: Intertextuality and Individualism in *Apocryphon of John* 1,5 – 2,19', in *Wilderness in Early Judaism and Christianity*, ed. F. Amsler and K. Fowler, Publications de l'institut romand des sciences bibliques 9 (Lausanne: Éditions du Zèbre, forthcoming), 147–73.
5 J. Rüpke, *On Roman Religion: Lived Religion and the Individual in Ancient Rome* (Ithaca and London: Cornell University Press, 2016), 7.
6 L. Siedentop, *Inventing the Individual: The Origins of Western Liberalism* (London: Allen Lane, 2014), 68–69.
7 Taylor, *A Secular Age*, 473–95; and R. N. Bellah et al., *Habits of the Heart: Individualism and Commitment in American Life*, with a new introduction, 1st California paperback edn (Berkeley: University of California Press, 2008), 142–63.
8 Rüpke, *On Roman Religion*, 5.

Bibliography

Ali, M. B. '"The Ruler" in the Fourth Gospel'. *Biblica et Patristica Thoruniensia* 12 (2019): 16–22.
Ascough, R. A., P. A. Harland, and J. S. Kloppenborg. *Associations in the Greco-Roman World*. Accessed January 23, 2022. http://www.philipharland.com/greco-roman-associations/
Balch, D. E., and C. Osiek. *Families in the New Testament World: Households and House Churches*. Louisville: Westminster/John Knox, 1997.
Barrett, C. K. *The Gospel According to John: An Introduction with Commentary and Notes on the Greek Text*. 2nd edn. London: SPCK, 1978.
Bauckham, R. J. *Gospel of Glory: Major Themes in Johannine Theology*. Grand Rapids: Baker Academic, 2015.
Beasley-Murray, *John*. WBC 36. Waco: Word, 1987.
Bellah, R. N., et al. *Habits of the Heart: Individualism and Commitment in American Life*. 1st California paperback edn. Berkeley: University of California Press, 2008.
Bennema, C. 'Judas the Betrayer: The Black Sheep of the Family'. In *Character Studies in the Fourth Gospel: Narrative Approaches to Seventy Figures in John*, edited by S. A. Hunt, D. F. Tolmie, and R. Zimmermann, 360–372. WUNT 314. Tübingen: Mohr-Siebeck, 2013.
Bohak, G. *Ancient Jewish Magic: A History*. Cambridge: Cambridge University Press, 2008.
Broadhead, E. K. 'Echoes of an Exorcism in the Fourth Gospel?'. *ZNW* 86 (1995): 111–119.
Brown, R. *The Gospel According to John*. 2 vols. AB 29. Garden City: Doubleday, 1964.
Bultmann, R. *The Gospel of John: A Commentary*. Translated by G. R. Beasley-Murray. Oxford: Basil Blackwell, 1971.
Burridge, R. A. *Imitatating Jesus: An Inclusive Approach to New Testament Ethics*. Grand Rapids, MI: Wm B. Eerdmans, 2007.
Busch, P. *Das Testament Salomos: Die älteste christliche Dämonologie, kommentiert und in deutscher Erstübersetzung*. TU 153. Berlin: Walter de Gruyter, 2006.
Caragounis, C. '"Abide in Me": The New Mode of Relationship between Jesus and His Followers as a Basis for Christian Ethics (John 15)'. In *Rethinking the Ethics of John: "Implicit Ethics" in the Johannine Writings*, edited by J. G. van der Watt and R. Zimmermann, 250–263. WUNT 291. Tübingen: Mohr Siebeck, 2012.

Carrithers, M. *Why Humans Have Cultures: Explaining Anthropology and Social Diversity*. Oxford: Oxford University Press, 1992.

Carson, D. A. *The Gospel According to John*. Leicester: Inter-Varsity Press; Grand Rapids: William B. Eerdmans, 1991.

Chepel, E. 'Invocations of the Blood of Christ in Greek Magical Amulets'. *Scrinium* 13 (2017): 53–71.

Colwell, E. C. 'A Definite Rule for the Use of the Article in the Greek New Testament'. *JBL* 52 (1933): 12–21.

Culpepper, R. A. *Anatomy of the Fourth Gospel: A Study in Literary Design*. Philadelphia: Fortress, 1983.

Dancygier, B., and E. Sweetser. *Figurative Language*. Cambridge Textbooks in Linguistics. Cambridge: Cambridge University Press, 2014.

Davies, P. R., G. J. Brooke, and P. R. Calloway. *The Complete World of the Dead Sea Scrolls*. London: Thames & Hudson, 2002.

Dennis, J. 'The "Lifting Up of the Son of Man" and the Dethroning of the "Ruler of this World": Jesus' Death as the Defeat of the Devil in John 12,31–32'. In *The Death of Jesus in the Fourth Gospel*, edited by G. Van Belle, 677–691. BETL 200. Leuven: Peeters-Leuven, 2007.

Edwards, M. J. *John*. Blackwell Bible Commentaries. Oxford: Blackwell Publishing, 2004.

Eggins, S. *An Introduction to Systemic Functional Linguistics*. 2nd edn. London: Bloomsbury Academic, 2004.

Ehrman, B. D., ed. *The Apostolic Fathers*. Vol. 1. LCL 24. Cambridge, MA: Harvard University Press, 2003.

Esler, P. F., and R. A. Piper. *Lazarus, Mary and Martha: A Social-Scientific and Theological Reading of John*. London: SCM, 2006.

Fairclough, N. *Discourse and Social Change*. Cambridge: Polity, 1992.

Fairclough, N. *Critical Discourse Analysis: The Critical Study of Language*. 2nd edn. London and New York: Routledge, 2013.

Fairclough, N. *Language and Power*. 3rd edn. London and New York: Routledge, 2015.

Fauconnier, G., and M. Turner. *The Way We Think: Conceptual Blending and the Mind's Hidden Complexities*. New York: Basic Books, 2002.

Ford, D. F. *The Gospel of John: A Theological Commentary*. Grand Rapids, MI: Baker Academic, 2021.

Fowler, R. *Linguistic Criticism*. 2nd edn. Oxford: Oxford University Press, 1996.

Griffith-Jones, R. 'Apocalyptic Mystagogy: Rebirth-from-above in the Reception of John's Gospel'. In *John's Gospel and Intimations of Apocalyptic*, edited by C. H. Williams and C. Rowland, 274–299. London: Bloomsbury, 2013.

Halliday, M. A. K., and C. Matthiessen. *Halliday's Introduction to Functional Grammar*. 4th edn. London: Routledge, 2014.

Harland, P. A. *Associations, Synagogues, and Congregations: Claiming a Place in Ancient Mediterranean Society*. Minneapolis: Fortress Press, 2003.

Hatch, E., and H. Redpath. *A Concordance to the Septuagint and the Other Greek Versions of the Old Testament (Including the Apocryphal Books)*. Vol. 2. Oxford: Clarendon Press, 1897.

Hill, C. E. *The Johannine Corpus in the Early Church*. Oxford: Oxford University Press, 2004.

Institute for New Testament Textual Research, ed. *Novum Testamentum Graece*. 28th revised edition. Stuttgart: Deutche Bibelgesellschaft, 2012.
Johnson, L. T. *Religious Experience in Earliest Christianity*. Minneapolis: Fortress Press, 1998.
Johnson, M. *The Meaning of the Body: Aesthetics of Human Understanding*. Cambridge: Cambridge University Press, 2007.
Kapferer, B. *A Celebration of Demons: Exorcism and the Aesthetic of Healing in Sri Lanka*. 2nd edn. Providence, R. I.: Berg; Washington, D. C.: Smithsonian Institution Press, 1991.
Kazen, T. *Jesus and Purity Halakhah: Was Jesus Indifferent to Impurity?* CB/NTS 38. Stockholm: Almqvist & Wiksell, 2002.
Keefer, K. 'Review of *The Johannine Corpus in the Early Church*, by Charles E. Hill'. *JBL* 124 (2005): 187–189.
King, K. L. 'The Place of the *Gospel of Philip* in the Context of Early Christian Claims about Jesus' Marital Status'. *NTS* 59.4 (2013): 565–587.
Klassen, W. *Judas: Betrayer or Friend of Jesus*. Minneapolis: Fortress, 1996.
Kloppenborg, J. S. *Christ's Associations: Connecting and Belonging in the Ancient City*. New Haven: Yale University Press, 2019.
Klutz, T. E. 'From Temple to Desert: Intertextuality and Individualism in *Apocryphon of John* 1,5 – 2,19'. In *Wilderness in Early Judaism and Christianity*, edited by F. Amsler and K. Fowler, 147–173. PIRSB 9. Lausanne: Éditions du Zèbre, forthcoming.
Klutz, T. E. *The Exorcism Stories in Luke-Acts: A Sociostylistic Reading*. SNTSMS 129. Cambridge: Cambridge University Press, 2004.
Klutz, T. E. *Rewriting the Testament of Solomon*. LSTS 53. London: T & T Clark, 2005.
Klutz, T. E. 'Inside the Bridal Chamber: Individual, Group and Intertextuality in *Gospel of Philip* 65.1–26'. In *Scripture as Social Discourse: Social-Scientific Perspectives on Early Jewish and Christian Writings*, edited by J. M. Keady, T. E. Klutz, and C. A. Strine, 211–232. London: T & T Clark, 2018.
Kobel, E. *Dining with John: Communal Meals and Identity Formation in the Fourth Gospel and its Historical and Cultural Context*. Biblical Interpretation 109. Leiden: E. J. Brill, 2011.
Kovacs, J. '"Now Shall the Ruler of This World Be Driven Out": Jesus' Death as Cosmic Battle in John 12:20-36'. *JBL* 114.2 (1995): 227–247.
La Potterie, I. de. 'L'exaltation du Fils de l'homme'. *Gregorianum* 49.3 (1968): 460–478.
Lakoff, G., and M. Johnson. *Metaphors We Live By*. Chicago: University of Chicago Press, 1980.
Lakoff, G., and M. Johnson. *Philosophy in the Flesh: The Embodied Mind and Its Challenge to Modern Thought*. New York: Basic Books, 1999.
Lamb, D. A. *Text, Context and the Johannine Community: A Sociolinguistic Analysis of the Johannine Writings*. LNTS 477. London: Bloomsbury T & T Clark, 2014.
Leech, G. N. *The Principles of Pragmatics*. London and New York: Longman, 1983.
Leonhardt-Balzer, L. 'The Ruler of the World, Antichrists, and Pseudo-Prophets: Johannine Variations on an Apocalyptic Motif'. In *John's Gospel and Intimations of Apocalyptic*, edited by C. H. Williams and C. Rowland, 180–199. London: Bloomsbury, 2013.

Levine, B. A. *In the Presence of the Lord: A Study of Cult and Some Cultic Terms in Ancient Israel*. SJLA 5. Leiden: E. J. Brill, 1974.

Levinson, S. *Pragmatics*. Cambridge Textbooks in Linguistics. Cambridge: Cambridge University Press, 1983.

Lightfoot, J. B., and J. R. Harmer, ed. *The Apostolic Fathers: Revised Greek Texts with Introductions and English Translations*. London: Macmillan and Co., 1891.

Lincoln, A. T. *The Gospel According to Saint John*. Peabody: Hendrickson; London: Continuum, 2005.

Lindars, B. 'Rebuking the Spirit: A New Analysis of the Lazarus Story of John 11'. *NTS* 38 (1992): 89–104.

Louw, J. P., and E. A. Nida. *Greek-English Lexicon of the New Testament Based on Semantic Domains*. 2nd edn, vol. I. New York: United Bible Societies, 1989.

Lundhaug H. *Images of Rebirth: Cognitive Poetics and Transformational Soteriology in the* Gospel of Philip *and the* Exegesis on the Soul. NHMS 73. Leiden: Brill, 2010.

Malherbe, A. J. *Social Aspects of Early Christianity*. 2nd edn. Philadelphia: Fortress Press, 1983.

Malina, B. J. 'Feast'. In *Biblical Social Values and Their Meaning*, edited by B. J. Malina and J. Pilch, 76–79. Peabody, MA: Hendrickson, 1993.

Malina, B. J. *The New Testament World: Insights from Cultural Anthropology*. 3rd edn. Louisville: Westminster/John Knox, 2001.

Martin, D. B. *The Corinthian Body*. New Haven: Yale University Press, 1995.

Martin, M. W. *Judas and the Rhetoric of Comparison in the Fourth Gospel*. New Testament Monographs 25. Sheffield: Sheffield Phoenix Press, 2010.

Mayer, W., and P. Allen. 'John Chrysostom'. In *The Early Christian World*, edited by P. F. Esler, 1054–1071. 2nd edn. London: Routledge, 2017.

Mazza, R. 'P. Ryl. Greek Add. 1166: Christian Prayer Amulet with a Tax Receipt on the Back'. *ZPE* 197 (2016): 73–84.

McHugh, J. 'Review of *Die Erhöhung und Verherrlichung Jesu im Johannesevangelium*, by W. Thüsing'. *CBQ* 22.4 (1960): 461–463.

Meyer, M., and R. Smith, ed. *Ancient Christian Magic: Coptic Texts of Ritual Power*. San Francisco: HarperCollins, 1994.

Moloney, F. *Signs and Shadows: Reading John 5–12*. Minneapolis: Fortress, 1996.

Moloney, F. *Glory not Dishonor: Reading John 13–21*. Minneapolis: Fortress, 1998.

Morschauser, S. N. 'Using History: Reflections on the Bentresh Stela'. *Studien zur Altägyptischen Kultur* 15 (1988): 203–223.

Moscicke, H. M. 'The Gerasene Exorcism and Jesus' Eschatological Expulsion of Cosmic Powers: Echoes of Second Temple Scapegoat Traditions in Mark 5.1-20'. *JSNT* 41.3 (2019): 363–383.

Most, G. W. 'The Judas of the Gospels and the *Gospel of Judas*'. In *The Gospel of Judas in Context*: *Proceedings of the First International Congress on the Gospel of Judas, Paris, Sorbonne*, October 27th–28th 2006, edited by M. Scopello, 69–80. Leiden: E. J. Brill, 2008.

Moule, C. F. D. *An Idiom Book of New Testament Greek*. 2nd edn. Cambridge: Cambridge University Press, 1959.

Moule, C. F. D. 'The Individualism of the Fourth Gospel'. *NovT* 5 (1962): 171–190.

Neyrey, J. *The Gospel of John in Cultural and Rhetorical Perspective*. Grand Rapids: Eerdmans, 2009.

Pagels, E. *The Origin of Satan*. London: Penguin, 1995.
Piper, R. A. 'Satan, Demons, and the Absence of Exorcism in the Fourth Gospel'. In *Christology, Controversy, and Community: New Testament Essays in Honour of David R. Catchpole*, edited by D. G. Horrell and C. M. Tuckett, 253–278. Leiden: Brill, 2000.
Plumer, E. 'The Absence of Exorcisms in the Fourth Gospel'. *Biblica* 78 (1997): 350–368.
Porter, S. E. *Idioms of the Greek New Testament*. Biblical Languages: Greek, 2. Sheffield: JSOT Press, 1992.
Porter, S. E. 'Is Critical Discourse Analysis Critical?' In *Discourse Analysis and the New Testament: Approaches and Results*, edited by S. E. Porter and J. T. Reed, 47–70. LNTS 170. Sheffield: Sheffield Academic Press, 1999.
Pratscher, W. 'Judas Iskariot im Neuen Testament und im Judasevangelium'. *NovT* 52 (2010): 1–23.
Reinhartz, A. *The Word in the World: The Cosmological Tale in the Fourth Gospel*. SBLMS 42. Atlanta: Scholars Press, 1992.
Reinhartz, A. 'The Jews of the Fourth Gospel'. In *The Oxford Handbook of Johannine Studies*, edited by J. M. Lieu and M. C. de Boer, 121–137. Oxford: Oxford University Press, 2018.
Renger, A.-B. 'The Ambiguity of Jesus: On the Mythicity of a New Testament Figure'. *Literature and Theology* 27.1 (2013): 1–17.
Riley, G. J. 'Devil'. In *Dictionary of Deities and Demons in the Bible*, edited by K. van der Toorn, B. Becking, and P. W. van der Horst, cols. 463–473. Leiden: E. J. Brill, 1995.
Robinson, J. M. *The Secrets of Judas*. New York: HarperCollins, 2006.
Rüpke, J. *On Roman Religion: Lived Religion and the Individual in Ancient Rome*. Ithaca and London: Cornell University Press, 2016.
Schnackenburg, R. *The Gospel according to John*. Vol. 2. Translated by Cecily Hastings et al. HTKNT. Tunbridge Wells, Kent: Burns & Oates, 1971.
Schnelle, U. *Das Evangelium nach Johannes*. 4th edn. THzNT 4. Leipzig: Evangelische Verlagsanstalt, 2009.
Schoedel, W. R. *Ignatius of Antioch: A Commentary on the Letters of Ignatius of Antioch*. Hermeneia. Philadelphia: Fortress, 1985.
Siedentop, L. *Inventing the Individual: The Origins of Western Liberalism*. London: Allen Lane, 2014.
Smith, D. E. *From Symposium to Eucharist: The Banquet in the Early Christian World*. Minneapolis: Fortress Press, 2003.
Smith, J. Z. 'Towards Interpreting the Demonic Powers in Hellenistic and Roman Antiquity'. *ANRW* II.16.1, 425–439.
Smith, J. Z. 'Trading Places'. In *Ancient Magic and Ritual Power*, edited by M. W. Meyer and P. A. Mirecki, 13–27. Leiden: E. J. Brill, 1995.
Sproston, W. 'Satan in the Fourth Gospel'. In *Studia Biblica 1978, II. Papers on the Gospels, Sixth International Congress on Biblical Studies, Oxford 3–7 April 1978*, edited by E. A. Livingstone, 307–311. Sheffield: JSOT, 1980.
Statham, S. *Critical Discourse Analysis: A Practical Introduction to Power in Language*. London: Routledge, 2022.
Steiner, G. *After Babel: Aspects of Language and Translation*. 3rd edn. Oxford: Oxford University Press, 1998.

Stuckenbruck, L. T. 'Evil in Johannine and Apocalyptic Perspective: Petition for Protection in John 17'. In *John's Gospel and Intimations of Apocalyptic*, edited by C. H. Williams and C. Rowland, 200–232. Bloomsbury T&T Clark, 2013.

Taussig, H. *In the Beginning Was the Meal: Social Experimentation and Early Christian Identity*. Minneapolis: Fortress, 2009.

Taylor, C. *A Secular Age*. Cambridge, MA: The Belknap Press, 2007.

Thatcher, T. 'Jesus, Judas, and Peter: Character by Contrast in the Fourth Gospel'. *BSac* 153 (1996): 435–448.

Thatcher, T. *Greater Than Caesar: Christology and Empire in the Fourth Gospel*. Minneapolis: Fortress, 2008.

Thiselton, A. C. *The First Epistle to the Corinthians*. NIGTC. Grand Rapids: William B. Eerdmans, 2000.

Thomas, J. C. *Footwashing in John 13 and the Johannine Community*. 2nd edn. Cleveland, TN: CPT Press, 2014.

Thüsing, W. *Die Erhöhung und Verherrlichung Jesu im Johannesevangelium*. 2nd edn, NTAbh 21.1. Münster: Aschendorff, 1970.

Thyen, H. *Das Johannes-evangelium*. HzNT 6. Tübingen: Mohr-Siebeck, 2005.

Turner, M. L. *The Gospel according to Philip: The Sources and Coherence of an Early Christian Collection*. NHMS 38. Leiden: Brill, 1996.

Turner, V. W. *The Forest of Symbols: Aspects of Ndembu Ritual*. Ithaca: Cornell University Press, 1967.

Turner, V. W. *The Ritual Process: Structure and Anti-Structure*. Harmondsworth: Penguin, 1969.

Turner, V. W. *Dramas, Fields, and Metaphors: Symbolic Action in Human Society*. Ithaca: Cornell University Press, 1974.

Twelftree, G. H. *In the Name of Jesus: Exorcism among Early Christians*. Grand Rapids: Baker, 2007.

Unterman, J. 'Passover'. In *Harper's Bible Dictionary*, edited by P. Achtemeier, 753–755. San Francisco: Harper, 1985.

Uro, R. *Ritual and Christian Beginnings: A Socio-Cognitive Analysis*. Oxford: Oxford University Press, 2016.

Uro, R. 'Ritual and the Rise of the Early Christian Movement'. In *The Early Christian World*, edited by P. F. Esler, 427–441. 2nd edn. London: Routledge, 2017.

van Gennep, A. *Rites of Passage*. Translated by M. B. Vizedom and G. L. Caffee. Chicago: University of Chicago Press, 1961.

van Oudtshoorn, A. 'Where Have All the Demons Gone? The Role and Place of the Devil in the Gospel of John'. *Neotestamentica* 51 (2017): 65–82.

Wallace, D. B. *Greek Grammar Beyond the Basics: An Exegetical Syntax of the New Testament*. Grand Rapids: Zondervan, 1996.

Watson, F. *What Is a Gospel?* Grand Rapids: Wm. B. Eerdmans, 2022.

Wengst, K. *Das Johannes-evangelium, 2. Teilband: Kapitel 11–21*. 2nd edn. TKNT. Stuttgart: Verlag W. Kohlhammer, 2001.

Wright, N. T., with J. P. Davies, 'John, Jesus, and "The Ruler of This World": Demonic Politics in the Fourth Gospel'. In *Conception, Reception, and the Spirit: Essays in Honour of Andrew T. Lincoln*, edited by J. G. McConville and L. K. Pietersen, 71–89. Eugene, OR: Cascade, 2015.

Wright, W. M. 'Greco-Roman Character Typing and the Presentation of Judas in the Fourth Gospel'. *CBQ* 71.3 (2009): 544–559.

Index

Page numbers followed by "n" indicate notes.

agency of demoniacs 51.
  See also demoniacs
ambiguity 21, 37, 51, 52, 54n20, 58n60, 71, 72, 80n38; of footwashing 71; of prophecy 52
amulets 76, 83n62, 88
apotropaic strategy 19, 47, 70–76, 86–88
Asmodaios 36, 40, 46
associations 5, 11, 48, 60–70, 78n16, 92; banquets 5, 32n60, 61, 63–70, 77, 79n22, 88–89; bouncers 67, 79n25; discipline and order 32n59, 43, 44, 61, 67, 80n35; rules 63–66; witnesses of rule-breaking 62

Barrett, Charles Kingsley 4, 8n10, 25n5, 26n10, 29n41, 56n44, 79n31
Bauckham, Richard A. 92
Beelzebul Controversy 20
Bellah, Robert N. 93
betrayal 15, 19, 31–32n58, 42, 57n49, 65, 69, 71, 78n16, 78n18, 80n37
body 32n60, 43–44, 58n60, 76; literal 22, 25, 43; metaphorical (i.e., social) 24, 31n55, 43–45
bread 17, 38–45, 54–55nn24–26, 55n32, 56n45, 68–69, 82n46, 86
bread-of-life 61–62, 88
Brown, Raymond 4, 25n1, 33n64, 42, 52n3, 79n31
Bultmann, Rudolf 4, 29n41–42, 53n3
Burridge, Richard A. 79n23

Carson, Donald A. 4, 53n3, 54n21, 57n48, 59n61
challenge and riposte 62–63, 69–70, 77n8, 88
chiasm 25
collectivism 3–4, 22, 92–93
collocation 15, 17, 18, 19, 20, 24, 26n17, 28n29, 38, 74, 78n12
community 3, 68, 79n22; of Christ followers 3, 22, 64, 87; Corinthian 65; Johannine 32n60, 67, 78n16; Qumran 63–64
Community Rule (1QS) 63–65
conceptual blending 23, 42, 50, 59n67, 73, 74, 81n42, 87
conceptual metaphor theory 6, 12–14, 56n36
container logic 22–24, 30n50
costly signalling 62–63, 69
Critical Discourse Analysis 5, 9n23, 14, 84
crucifixion 1, 13, 26n16–17
Culpepper, R. Alan 28n30–31

darkness 24, 39, 46, 58n59, 89
demon 12, 14–21, 23, 27n24, 29n38, 29n40, 30n45, 36, 40, 47, 51, 58n59, 72, 74–76, 85, 88–91
demoniacs 36–40, 53n11, 90–91.
  See also agency of demoniacs
demonology 14–18, 23
destination of expelled spirits 46, 89
devil 1, 2, 7n3, 10–20, 24, 27n24, 27n26, 29n32, 30n47, 32n62,

32n64, 75, 87, 90; murderer 16, 28n30, 39. See also Satan
dirt 25, 32n60, 43–44

emperor 11
Essenes 64
eucharist 11, 32n60, 38–45, 47–48, 55n32, 58n60, 66, 73–77, 79n22, 81n42, 82n46, 82n48, 83n62, 87–88; unworthy reception 31n55, 75, 87
exorcism 2, 5, 21, 34, 43, 46, 70, 84, 87; absence in Fourth Gospel 2, 35, 85, 90; agency 37, 53–54n19; cleansing 43, 48–50, 59n67, 86; commands 19–20, 29nn38–41, 48, 49; cosmic 35; definition of 7n9, 35–36, 73, 81n45, 88, 90; materials 40–41, 86; phasing and structure of 72–73; Sinhalese 68; Synoptic 12, 20, 29n43, 30n45, 36–37, 51, 90–91; technique of 37–38
experiential distance 41–42, 56n37, 56n38

Fairclough, Norman 5
faith 16, 28n31, 37, 53n16, 56n44, 86–87, 90–93
food 38–40, 54n24, 68–69, 72, 80n33, 87
footwashing 18, 23, 25, 26n16, 31n55, 32n60, 42–45, 48–49, 51, 59n67, 86
Ford, David F. 59n62
free-riders 69, 92

glory 25, 29n41, 70, 72, 74
Gospel of Philip 74–75

Halliday, M. A. K. 5
Harland, Philip A. 60, 78n20
honour 19, 42, 62–63, 65, 68–70, 77n8, 77n9, 88

'I am' 46, 90
Ignatius of Antioch 73–74, 81n43, 82n46
imperial rule 11, 46, 57n51
individualism 90–93
insults 62–64, 80n38, 88
Iobacchoi 65–66, 68, 89

Jesus 1–2, 5, 12–13, 15, 19–22, 37–38, 45, 49, 61, 69–72, 85, 89–90; arrest of 46, 55n30, 57n48, 57n49, 79n25; death of 13, 19, 26n16, 28n28; feet of 18, 62–63; as prophet 2, 17, 23, 24–25, 30n46, 40, 50, 52, 64, 84–85, 88
John Chrysostom 75–76
Johnson, Mark 6, 7n7, 12–13, 22, 30n50, 53n9, 56n36
Josephus 64
Judas 2–6, 10–11, 21, 36, 43, 46, 48, 51–52, 61–63, 71–72, 84–86, 88; as betrayer 19, 65, 80n37; as container of Satanic ruler 11, 20–24, 50, 54n19, 90, 91; diabolical association of 15–19, 30n47, 33n64, 86; discursive prominence of 24, 28n30, 37, 47, 58n54; exclusion/expulsion of 13, 18, 20, 22, 38, 44–45, 47, 54n21, 64, 67, 69–70, 78n12, 86, 92; as liar 16, 18, 29n32; as murderer 76; symbolic character of 91–92; as unbeliever 16, 17, 23, 37, 45, 86; uncleanness of 23, 42–44, 49, 51, 59n64, 86, 90; as unproductive vine 50, 69

Kapferer, Bruce 68, 72–73
Kloppenborg, John S. 80n35
Klutz, Todd E. 29n38, 53n8, 53n15
Kobel, Esther 31n58, 78n16
Kovacs, Judith 7n10

Lakoff, George 6, 7n7, 12–13, 22, 30n50, 53n9, 56n36
Lazarus 17–19, 28n31, 62
Leonhardt-Balzer, Jutta 26n13, 31n54
lexical strings 4, 5, 18–19, 28n30, 29n41, 33n65, 48, 57n48, 74
Lincoln, Andrew T. 4, 28n28, 53n10
Lord's Supper 60, 87.
    See also eucharist
LXX 39, 47, 58n59

magic 34–35, 52n2
Martin, Michael 29n41, 59n64
Martha (sister of Mary and Lazarus) 17–18, 28n31, 62
Mary (sister of Martha and Lazarus) 17–19, 28n31, 29n32, 62–63

meals 4–5, 17–20, 28n28, 32n60, 38–40, 43–44, 48, 55n27, 55n32, 60–70, 72, 77, 86, 88; order of service 48, 67–68, 79n26; portion size 5, 67–69
metaphor 12, 30n50, 43, 56n36; container metaphor 2, 6, 7n7, 8n10, 11, 14, 19–24, 30n48, 46, 54n19, 84, 90, 91; orientational metaphor 6, 12–13, 26n11, 46, 84
metaphorical coherence 6, 14–15, 47, 84
Moloney, Francis 4
morsel (of eucharist) 5, 21, 29n39, 38–42, 44–45, 47–48, 54n24, 55n32, 56n36, 56n45, 58n60, 66–69, 72–73, 80n33, 85–87; diminutive suffix 38–39, 54n24, 68, 79n31; discursive prominence of 38–39, 67; size 5, 67–69
Moule, C. F. D. 92

Neyrey, Jerome 29n32, 57n49

part-whole concept 43
passive voice 37, 50, 54n19
Peter (apostle) 57n49, 67, 71, 79n25, 80n37
Philo of Alexandria 64, 78n13
Piper, Ronald A. 7n4, 29n43
politeness 38, 80n38
prophecy-fulfilment scheme 4, 20–21, 24–25, 31n54, 43–44, 48, 50, 84, 87–90
protection against Satan 23, 32n59, 41, 47, 58n59, 67, 75–76, 87, 92
purification 3, 23–25, 31–32n58, 42–43, 49–50, 59n67, 86–87

reference chains 5–6, 20, 24, 47, 57n48
ritual 5, 28n28, 40, 62, 66, 69–72, 75, 77n7, 80n38, 88, 92; as paradigm 23, 38, 41–45, 87; of cosmic power 35, 52n2, 58n60, 87; of relocation 3, 23, 36, 42–47, 51–52, 59n67, 72, 78n12, 84, 86.

See also eucharist; Yom Kippur
ruler of this world 1–3, 5, 7n10, 10–14, 18, 20–25, 30n46, 32n62, 35, 39, 46–47, 57n51, 84–90. *See also* devil; Satan
Rüpke, Jörg 92

Satan 1–3, 6, 10–12, 19–20, 22–24, 33n64, 35–36, 39, 45, 57n51, 65, 74, 85, 87m, 89, 91; fall of 2, 7n5, 12, 13. *See also* devil; ruler of this world
Saul (king of Israel) 39–40, 55nn27–30
Schnackenburg, Rudolf 3–4, 8n17
Schnelle, Udo 4, 30n46, 53n10
Siedentop, Larry 93
Smith, Dennis 68, 79n26, 80n33
Smith, Jonathan Z. 36
space 14–15, 43, 46, 57n49, 72, 89
spirit-possession 20, 23–24, 33n64, 36–37, 39, 45, 48, 53n16, 85, 87, 91
Statutes of the Iobacchoi 65–66

Taylor, Charles 52n1, 93
Therapeutae 64, 89
Thomas, John C. 32n60
Thüsing, Wilhelm 1, 3–4, 7n5, 8n17, 22–23, 27n17, 31n54, 84
Thyen, Hartwig 4, 32n63, 55n32, 79n31
Twelftree, Graham 73, 81n45

unbelief 11, 16, 17, 23, 25, 32n58, 45, 90, 92
uncleanness 42, 43, 75

verticality 1, 7n9, 13–15, 23, 58n55
vines and vineyard 23, 47–51, 59n62, 69, 92

wand of Dionysus 66–67, 79n21
witch of Endor 39
word of Jesus 11, 17, 20–21, 23, 25, 48–49, 58n52, 59n67, 85
world (i.e., the Johannine cosmos) 1–2, 43, 45–46, 90

Yom Kippur 36

For Product Safety Concerns and Information please contact our EU representative GPSR@taylorandfrancis.com
Taylor & Francis Verlag GmbH, Kaufingerstraße 24, 80331 München, Germany

www.ingramcontent.com/pod-product-compliance
Lightning Source LLC
Chambersburg PA
CBHW071823230426
43670CB00013B/2547